01 02 03 04 05 06 07
08 09 10 11 12 13 14
21
28
35
36 37 38 39 40 41 42
43 44 45 46 47 48 49
50 51 52 53 54 55 56
57 58 59 60 61 62 63
64 65 66 67 68 69 70
71 72 73 74 75 76 77
78 79 80 81 82 83 84
85 86 87 88 89 90

90 DAYS
TO YOUR NOVEL

A Day-by-Day Plan for
Outlining & Writing Your Book

WRITER'S DIGEST
BOOKS

WritersDigest.*com*
Cincinnati, Ohio

SARAH DOMET

To receive a free weekly e-mail newsletter delivering tips and updates about writing and about Writer's Digest products, register directly at http://newsletters.fwpublications.com.

18 17 16 15 14   9 8 7 6 5

Distributed in Canada by Fraser Direct
100 Armstrong Avenue
Georgetown, Ontario, Canada L7G 5S4
Tel: (905) 877-4411

Distributed in the U.K. and Europe by F+W Media International
Brunel House, Newton Abbot, Devon, TQ12 4PU, England
Tel: (+44) 1626-323200, Fax: (+44) 1626-323319
E-mail: postmaster@davidandcharles.co.uk

Distributed in Australia by Capricorn Link
P.O. Box 704, Windsor, NSW 2756 Australia
Tel: (02) 4577-3555

Library of Congress Cataloging-in-Publication Data
Domet, Sarah.
  90 days to your novel : a day-by-day plan for outlining & writing your book / by Sarah Domet.
    p. cm.
  ISBN 978-1-58297-997-7 (alk. paper)
  1. Fiction--Authorship. 2. Creative writing. I. Title.
  PN3365.D57 2010
  808.3--dc22
                                    2010022095

Edited by Scott Francis
Designed by Claudean Wheeler
Cover illustration by Gregor909/iStockphoto.com
Production coordinated by Debbie Thomas

Dedication

For my parents, Luke and Sally, who taught me life is a story; be proud of the pages you write.

Table of Contents

AN INTRODUCTION, A CHALLENGE, AND A WARNING

So you think you can write a novel, huh?

The difference between a novelist and a would-be novelist is that one person actually writes while the other person simply *talks* about writing. Which one are you?

One person romanticizes the idea of being a writer—perhaps swilling some cognac in a moody red-lit coffee shop (dark-framed glasses and argyle sweater vest optional in this vision), pen hoisted in air, waiting for that old muse, Inspiration, to hit. The other realizes that writing is rather, shall we say, *unsexy*; there is nothing particularly spectacular about sitting in front of a computer, *alone*, pulling out your hair, wildly scribbling notes, regretfully saying "no" to that dinner invitation from your friends to try that fabulous new restaurant in town because you just *have* to finish this scene. In the fever of your writing, you feel your characters need you more than your friends do now ... and, well, another evening spent alone with the page. How's that for romantic?

So you think you're a writer. That's why you're here, no doubt. If you've picked up this book, chances are you have a vision for a novel or perhaps a fantastic plot conceit or a compelling character. But are you willing to do the work?

Are you willing to trade the *idea* of being a writer for the *habits* that any successful writer must adopt?

Or maybe you're just waiting for inspiration to hit. Let me guess: When it does, you'll waste no time in that frenzied fugue state, typing out your novel, from start to finish. The problem is, inspiration hits you only in fits and spurts now—perhaps when you're driving or walking the dog or sitting in your cubical at work or inhaling a pesto chicken wrap during your lunch break. This inspiration never sticks around long enough to compel you to write the entire novel—maybe only a paragraph or a scene here and there. Maybe it's really less a novel and more a jumble of ideas. But someday, right?

If you've come to this book looking for inspiration, I'm going to give you your first dose of cold, hard truth: Writing doesn't require large doses of inspiration. Writers who wait for inspiration to hit, particularly writers with other full-time commitments—a job, a family, a needy feline companion named Ponce de Leon—will likely find themselves waiting forever. They'll find themselves sitting in coffee shops, pens poised in air, ordering another drink, looking around, talking to the locals (who saw the notebook and pen, and thus believe some writing was surely done that day), picking some lint off that argyle sweater, and then packing up to go home and watch another episode of *Seinfeld* on TV. That's reality.

Frankly, I'm tired of writers talking only about inspiration. I'm sick of books that help you find the creative inner you, the idea that will spark that spark and finally compel you to write your novel. Novel writing isn't always about finding the right ideas. It's about finding the time and the energy. I'm a pragmatist when it comes to writing, so if you're looking for some of that touchy-feely New

Agey writer speak, you won't find it in these pages. Instead you'll find a practical approach, one that requires you to stop talking and start writing.

Self-taught fiction writer Octavia Butler once noted, "Forget inspiration. Habit is more dependable. Habit will sustain you whether you're inspired or not. Habit will help you finish and polish your stories. Inspiration won't. Habit is *persistence in practice*." (Emphasis mine.) Yes, inspiration might contain the spark and life of your idea, but habit gets the writing done. Inspiration resides in your heart; habit resides in your fingers. Inspiration propels; habit completes. Art equals habit plus inspiration. It's a simple equation.

If you do a quick Internet search for "workout videos," chances are you'll find DVDs with such titles as *8-Minute Abs Like Stonehenge, 30 Days to a Teeny Tummy and a Tiny Hiney,* or *The 10-Minute Shrinking-Self Solution.* All these titles hope to persuade you that with a bit of daily persistence, you can become that muscle-toned individual on the front of the DVD cover. The amazing thing about these videos is that they work! Who knew? When one routinely exercises, instead of offering up excuses (like I do), who would have guessed that he or she looks and feels better about themselves? Sure, you may not have biceps like the Incredible Hulk, but they're better than you've ever seen on those thin arms of yours. Yet the daily dedication is the hard part. It's just too easy to skip a workout here or there—to choose leisure over work. (Or, let's face it, to choose work over work.)

Here's something to think about: Your mind is a muscle, too—and writing, much like exercising, requires that persistence-in-practice if you hope to make the progress necessary to finish a novel. You're going to have to write.

Every day. Isn't that what a writer is, after all? Someone who writes?

90 Days to Your Novel is a challenge to anyone who always said they wanted to write a book, but "never found the time" to sit down and do the work. Admittedly, it's difficult to write without a deadline. This book is the deadline, the impetus, and the framework you will need to get your novel written. This book is a practical guide that will lead you from the initial stages of brainstorming your novel, through the developmental stages of outlining, and into the final stages of writing your first draft. And, most importantly, it will keep you on schedule, giving you specific assignments and points of focus each day to help you compartmentalize your novel. That's the trick of any large project, after all—biting off one small chunk at a time.

The premise of *90 Days to Your Novel* is based upon four driving philosophies.

1. If you do not write on a daily basis, or a near-daily basis, you are not a writer.
2. Outlining is an essential component of novel writing.
3. Novels are written scene by scene, not character by character or action by action.
4. It's possible to write a book in months, not years.

Sounds fairly straightforward, but this book requires something from you, the reader, too. First, it requires your commitment to sit down and write for *at least* two to three hours a day for the next ninety days, no excuses. Tell your family and friends you'll not be available for weekly movie marathons or vacations or major home-renovation projects or nights out on the town that will make you too tired the next day to write. You'll need to make sacrifices. For the next ninety days, you'll need to view writing as a job, and your payment will be the satisfaction you'll receive from your progress and, ultimately, your completion.

Secondly, in order to realistically write a draft in ninety days, you are going to have to critically assess your novel's ideas and components *before* writing. Therefore, the outlining process is going to be absolutely essential if you hope to make good progress in such a short space of time. I can hear the gripes already. Just the mention alone of the word *outline* strikes fear in the heart of many creative types. Many writers view outlines as a restrictive straight-jacket in an otherwise creative realm—or as unnecessary process work *they* don't need. If you have negative feelings about outlining, my suggestion is, kindly, this: Get over it. And quickly. Outlining is an excellent tool for plotting the arc of your novel and for ensuring you don't waste time on extraneous scenes that lend little in the way of support to your story. Furthermore, outlines can ensure that you have a balance and variety of scenes necessary to pace the novel and keep your readers' attention.

Joyce Carol Oates, one of the most talented and notably productive writers of our day, is notorious for her outlines, elaborate charts taped to the wall next to her writing desk. During a lecture she delivered at a writing conference I attended in Saratoga Springs in 2006, she was asked what it was like to be such a prolific writer, producing novel after novel after novel. Her response was both frank and humorous: She said, "I don't understand why most writers don't write *more!*" (I believe I quoted her correctly; I was too busy guffawing with my colleagues to write it down.) This is a woman who, after all, has written, to date, fifty-six novels, at the rate of two to three a year, not including a long list of short-story collections, poetry collections, children's fiction, and essays. Perhaps her outlining technique, part of her prewriting process, holds the secret to her abundant output. If I were a betting woman, I'd place my wager and up my ante.

Next, you must commit yourself to writing your novel scene by scene, from your outline, and in an orderly fashion. Though writing classes often discuss and teach fiction writing using the discrete elements of the craft—character, plot, setting, dialogue, and so forth—you'll need to focus on all these elements simultaneously through scene writing. You'll come to understand that these elements are interrelated: Character affects plot, which determines setting, which can reveal mood, tone, and voice. Though you may be tempted to jump forward and backward, focusing on the "good parts" and reworking your favorite moments, your novel will be best served if you approach it in a linear fashion. On the front end you should simply focus on pushing yourself to produce pages and completed scenes; on the back end you can worry about revising for your reader.

Finally, this book asks you to dispel any notions you may have that a novel takes years—even one year—to write. With dedication, foresight, and attention to time management, a novel can easily be penned in months, not years. Many authors, living and dead, have written their novels in a matter of months, sometimes even weeks. For example, Faulkner is purported to have written *As I Lay Dying* in only six weeks. Zora Neale Hurston wrote *Their Eyes Were Watching God* in just under two months. Joyce Carol Oates cranks out her novels at a breakneck pace, sometimes publishing two or three novels a year. While allotting ninety days for a solid first draft asks that you work quickly and diligently, it's certainly not the fastest a novel has ever been written. That is, I won't be asking you to reinvent the wheel here. Instead you'll be asked to follow the tried-and-tested schedule and writing assignments—and to put in a little extra elbow grease—to reach your end goal.

HOW TO USE THIS BOOK

This book is organized into two parts. Part I should be read *before* you begin the ninety-day challenge, and Part II can be read as you are completing it.

Part I describes several outlining techniques and the strengths/limitations of each. The goal is to allow you to find the best outlining technique to suit your needs. However, you'll soon recognize that all outlining approaches will eventually lead to the same place: a well-organized and structured novel with a clear narrative arc. Part I will also introduce you to the basics of scene writing and scene structure. You should read Part I before beginning the ninety-day writing challenge. Don't worry, the clock won't start until you are ready.

Part II is divided by days/weeks and should be read in sections as you progress through the ninety-day challenge. For the first three weeks, each day's lesson will address a specific component of novel writing and provide a specific assignment. These assignments will build upon one another, culminating in a solid first outline. In week four, you will be asked to assess the strengths and weaknesses of your outline as we explore in detail the arc of the novel. Week five will focus on developing both major and minor characters in your novel, choosing the best point of view and adjusting your outlines accordingly. Starting week six, this book will guide you in a linear fashion through the eight-week drafting process. Borrowing on the outline you generated, along with the various assignments you completed, we'll tackle the daunting task of writing the novel, one scene at a time. Don't worry; I'll be here to encourage you and keep you on task.

Writing is difficult. It's work. Hard work. It's understandable if you don't want to put yourself through the agony of becoming a writer. Maybe you should become a candlestick maker instead. Or a hat maker. Make something else, if you want: A sandwich, a soapbox derby car, a scarf and matching mittens. Novel writing is not for everyone, and certainly not for those who don't have the patience to sit down for countless hours staring at a computer screen. Certainly, there will be times in the next three months when you don't feel like writing, and you'll have to write anyway. There will be times when you feel as though you're writing drivel, and it might be, but you'll keep pushing yourself to write. There will be times when you face writer's block, or you are tired, or you don't know what to write, or you don't know how to describe what you want to say, or you grow tired of thinking of the same characters, or you don't know what your characters want or if you even like them—and you'll force yourself through these moments because that's what writers do: They write. I promise you the pages will add up, but only if you keep writing.

In famed journalist Malcolm Gladwell's book, *Outliers*, he claims that in order to be an "expert" at something, you must practice it for ten thousand hours. So, according to Gladwell, if you took to practicing writing as a full-time job (forty hours a week/fifty-two weeks), you'll achieve expert status in about five years. That's a lot of time. But this is good news for you, too. It means with practice, introspection, and a little bit (or a lot) of self-criticism, you'll become a stronger writer with each word you pen, each page you write. Good writers aren't born good writers; they develop into good writers through dedication and practice. Through hard work. Through habit.

So I'll say it again: Writing is difficult. All serious writers—the seasoned and the rookies—know this. But, it can also be exhilarating work. You know this already, and that's why you're here. You have a great novel idea—good characters, a compelling plot, a vivid setting—but perhaps you don't know where to start. Perhaps you're afraid of what will happen if you stop talking about being a writer and start writing. What might you discover?

90 Days to Your Novel is a line drawn in the sand with a challenge to cross it: On one side are the many folks who talk about being writers; on the other you'll find those humble, disciplined, intrepid souls who expend the creative energy—supported by a sturdy outline and generous amounts of lonely *time*—to become real writers. If you follow this book's advice, your reward will be simple: your very own novel in ninety days.

So you think you can write a novel? Prove it. Fill out the following contract, tear it out, and tape it next to your writing desk as a reminder of your commitment.

You have ninety days. The count starts when you say go. *On your mark, get set ...*

WRITING CONTRACT

Agreement made this _____ day of _____ in the year _____ whereby I, _____(FILL IN YOUR NAME)_____, do hereby commit myself to writing a minimum of two to three hours a day, every day, for ninety consecutive days, no excuses. The work will begin on the date I set forth in writing below.

I pledge to work diligently and habitually, even when I'm tired, hungry, cold, grouchy, or lonely, or have to get up early or stay up late, and/or even when I'd rather be doing something else. I am entering this agreement with myself because I recognize that the only way to write a novel is to dedicate myself to the project and to put in the necessary (solitary) time. I may or may not enjoy the process, but I also know there's a little bit of agony in writing. The pain I inflict upon myself shall be my own.

I will begin my novel on _____(FILL IN DATE)_____ and expect my first completed draft to be finished on _____ (FILL IN DATE)_____, approximately ninety days later. No penalty shall be found for failing to meet this mandated deadline, but the reward for meeting it shall be the satisfaction of having written my own novel. I shall blame no one but myself for the delays along the way.

This pledge is made with my full consent and awareness, and under no obligation to anyone but myself.

_____

(SIGNATURE)

Part 1:

OUTLINING TECHNIQUES
& SCENE-WRITING BASICS

CHOOSING YOUR TOOLS:
An Outlining Primer

All artists have their tools. For a painter, it's a paintbrush; for a photographer, it's a camera. For a novelist, it's an outline.

But not just anybody with a paintbrush or a camera is an artist. You must first learn how to use your artist's tool properly in order to create something that will invite others—complete strangers, most often—to spend time with what you've created, to think about it long after they've left the art gallery or museum. Or even after they've closed the book. That's the deepest hope of every serious artist—to create a lasting, thoughtful reflection on the human experience.

However, when some writers hear the word *outline*, they run screaming for the hills. These individuals believe that writing is about the process of discovery—that their characters reveal their personalities *through* the process of writing. And how, pray tell, can you know what a character will do before he has even done it?

My response: Yawn. Eye roll. Sigh. *Oh, petunias.* The line for excuse makers begins here: X. (Not that the excuse line actually leads anywhere. Plan on standing there for a while.)

As you may have guessed, I feel strongly about outlines. In the past, when I've taught college writing courses, I've had students initially resist outlining as though it were the most tedious task known to mankind. It was as though these students were poor Luke in the famous ditch-digging scene from *Cool Hand Luke,* where the haggard protagonist is ordered to dig "his dirt" out of Boss Keen's ditch, then to remove "his dirt" out of the prison yard and fill in the hole he'd just made. Through the process of digging and refilling the ditch, digging and refilling the ditch, and digging and refilling the ditch, feeble Luke's strengths and limitations are tested, as is his sanity. There was just no purpose to all that digging.

Outlining is nothing like this, of course.

Here are some common myths about outlining: Outlines eliminate the need to think through the writing process once you begin writing. Outlines are restrictive. There is only one correct way to write a proper outline. Outlines stunt creativity. Outlining is a painful process. Once you write an outline, you cannot stray from what you've written. Outlines are for individuals who can't organize thoughts in their heads or who don't know what they are doing. Outlines are used primarily by control freaks.

Why do some students hold such beliefs?

I remember back in grade school when Mrs. N__ taught my class the essentials of a proper outline. The lesson lasted an eternity: Use Roman numerals. Each heading and subheading must have at least two parts. Do not mix up the types and variety of outlines you use. You must use either complete sentences or sentence fragments—but only one and never both. You must use capital letters for main points, lowercase letters for subpoints, and numbers for sub-subpoints. Ack! Back then, Mrs. N__ taught us that there was only one proper way to write an outline, and it was just so. Day 2 into our outlining lesson, and the entire class had found the blessed release of sleep, heads resting heavily on our desks, exhausted by the rules and the sheer boredom of it all. Was it time for recess yet?

Luckily, we no longer sit at the mercy of our grade-school teachers. Mrs. N__'s ideas weren't wrong—maybe it was just her approach. (I don't blame Mrs. N___; in fact, I rather liked her.) Not everybody processes and utilizes information in the same manner, and so not all outlines will be equally effective for all individuals. A traditional outline might work for some, while a charted outline might work better for others. The trick is to find an outlining technique that jibes with your style and personality, with how you visualize your story line. Are you a more spatial learner? A visual one? Do you conceive of your novel's characters and events in a chronological fashion or in a nonlinear way? Are you a big-picture person or a detail-oriented thinker? These questions, and their answers, will help you determine which kind of outlining style will work best for you.

Once my college-writing students (reluctantly) found an outlining process that worked for them, these same individuals who griped and bellyached about being forced to compose an outline—oh, those outlines, scourge of all humanity!—sheepishly admitted that "well ... maybe it did help a little bit after all." And their grades showed it. No longer did their papers and narratives offer up rambling and unfocused ideas. No longer did they jump from thought to thought within the same paragraph or present their visions to a reader in an illogical or confusing fashion. Their characters become more complicated, their plotlines more developed, their stories more compelling.

The outlines worked.

Outlines are not just for beginning writers, though certainly fledgling novelists might benefit the most from them. Plenty of novelists, from all ranges in their careers, rely on the outline to help them generate a solid story. E.M. Forster, in his often-taught *Aspects of the Novel*, notes, "the basis of a novel is a story, and a story is a narrative of events arranged in time sequence." (Though, to be clear, Forster makes a clear distinction between story and plot, and we'll discuss this in a later section.) Outlines help us not only to generate stories, but to organize stories—to clarify (to the writer herself), before drafting the novel, when particular events happened within the context of the novel's time frame. Though you'll find plenty of examples of famous novelists who do not work closely with outlines—Stephen King, for one—you'll also find a plethora of writers who find outlining to be indispensable.

In this chapter, we'll examine the types and varieties of outlines you may find helpful in the writing process. I encourage you to experiment with each and to find the method that's most compatible with your own writing habits, your work space, or your processes. But keep in mind that each method is going to lead to the same place: a well-organized and structured outline with a clear narrative arc. You'll find no easy shortcuts. You'll conceive of your novel before you write a single word of your novel, and in this manner, you'll ensure you have your thoughts organized enough to complete your novel in ninety days.

You'll undertake this process work before you begin, of course, just as a long-distance runner prepares for a marathon with a regular series of shorter runs before the big race. And if you skip a lesson here or there, or don't spend the necessary time drafting and critiquing your outline, don't be surprised when you find can't finish your novel in ninety days. The secret to success, after all, is not your inspiration, remember, but your habits. In an interview, curmudgeonly humorist Andy Rooney once said, "My advice is not to wait to be struck by an idea. If you're a writer, you sit down and damn well decide to *have* an idea. That's the way to get an idea." This idea strikes a similar chord with novelist Margaret Atwood's thinking when she advises, "Put your left hand on the table. Put your right hand in the air. If you stay that way long enough, you'll get a plot." William Faulkner shares a similar sentiment: "I write only when I feel the inspiration. Fortunately, inspiration strikes at 10 o'clock everyday." None of these writers waits around for inspiration to light a fire beneath them. Instead they rely upon routine, upon self-determination. You should, too.

We'll be spending four weeks—yes, FOUR WEEKS!—developing our outlines, and while this may seem like an excessive amount of time to someone just itching to get started on her novel, remember: patience is key. Mr. Miyagi taught the Karate Kid martial arts by having him wax his car *(wax on, wax off)*, paint a fence, and scrub a deck, among other mundane household tasks. Writing a novel in ninety days will take equal parts diligence and patience. You must put your faith in the process. The racing ahead will only lead to the falling behind. *Ah, thank you, Mr. Miyagi. I see now.*

But before we even begin, it's important to remember this: Outlines change. People change. Characters change. Plots change. Even change changes.

I encourage you to think of an outline not as a paper map but as a personal tour guide taking you through an unknown terrain. "Can we go over there?" you might ask, pointing to a pristine spot off in the distance. When navigating by paper, you'll not be able to do so, as the area you've pointed out has not been marked on the map. When navigating with a tour guide, however, you'll get a different answer. "Yes, we can go there if you like, but the pathway is rather steep and narrow. You'll have to climb that jagged rock over there, too, and cross a rapid stream. You might be uncomfortable. Do you still want to go?" the tour guide asks. Yes. Yes, of course you do.

Outlines are not meant to strictly enforce adherence to one rigid perception of our novel. That's the myth. Instead think of your outline simply as a suggestion. Think of it, perhaps, as a recipe. Sure, you can follow a recipe for, say, a cheesecake exactly. Or you can add a bit of chocolate to the batter, and poof—chocolate cheesecake! Or, you can add some pecans, maple syrup, and rum, and you've got a different, delicious version of the same classic. Recipes guide us—but the creativity still belongs to the head chef.

As your novel progresses, you may find yourself editing your outline—and as your novel more fully develops, you might find yourself discarding your outline altogether. What's important, however, is that you take the necessary time to think through characters and plotlines to make sure your initial ideas are sustainable. Police detectives are required, by their job description, to follow all leads, even dead ones. Fortunately, novelists bear no such responsibility. In fact, the more time we spend up front eliminating flat characters and dead plotlines, the less time we'll waste during the writing process itself—and the more time you can dedicate to actually writing.

Think it's a great idea to write a novel about a young man who realized he has the magical power to generate solar energy though the touch of his hand? That'd be pretty interesting. What about a character who is allergic to all foods except pickled bologna and parsnips? Wouldn't that be a hoot? What about a woman who plays Mary in her small town's live manger scene during the holidays, even though she's Jewish? That'd be clever. But clever does not sustain a novel.

Testing your character and plot ideas—through the outlining process—will allow you to examine whether or not your idea is rich, compelling, and sustainable—or simply a clever notion that's better left for cocktail-hour conversation. "Hey, did you hear the one about ..."

Following are just a handful of outlining techniques that may work for you during your ninety-day writing challenge. Read through the descriptions and decide which is best suited for you.

THE "STRUCTURE-PLUS" OUTLINE

The structure-plus outline is the most traditional method of outlining presented here. In other words, it's the kind of outline that looks most similar to the outlining method you were likely taught in elementary school by Mrs. N___. These outlines contain detailed written descriptions of the individual scenes you'll be writing, which will progress in a linear fashion throughout your novel.

The most common kind of structural outline can be roughly divided into three parts, or three "acts," as they are often termed. We'll discuss the structure of a novel at length in a later section, but, in brief, Act I introduces (characters and plot situations), Act II complicates (character wants something, but plot complications stand in her way), and Act III resolves (character gets what she wants or doesn't get what she wants).

The "plus" in the structure-plus outline will ask you to name the setting of each scene, the characters involved, and the motivation or the purpose of the scene.

A structure-plus outline might look something like this:

I. **SETTING:** The back room at Spaghetti O'Plenty; 5:00 in the evening

CHARACTERS: Rhys, Trina, and Trina's manager at the restaurant

PURPOSE: To complicate the plot and build tension between Rhys and Trina

  a. Rhys gets his acceptance letter to a prestigious art school and, excited, goes to his girlfriend, Trina's, work with the intention of telling her.

    i. Trina goes on break and takes him to the back room.

    ii. "I need to tell you something," Trina says. "I'm pregnant."

    iii. Trina's manager interrupts, "Trina, we need you on Table 7."

  b. Rhys is shocked and can feel his dream of being a painter slipping away.

    i. "What are you going to do?" Rhys asks.

    ii. "Me? What am I going to do? We're in this together," Trina says, upset.

    iii. Trina's manager comes in and sees her crying. "Leave her alone and get out of here," he says. "Trina, I said Table 7."

  c. Rhys leaves the restaurant, crumpling up the letter and throwing it away on his way out.

The structure-plus outline is the most thorough of the outline varieties listed here. Drafting a structure-plus outline will likely take you more time on the front end, *before* you write your novel, but working with an outline of this nature can potentially save a tremendous amount of valuable time on the back end, *during* the writing of your novel. Remember, the more thinking you do up front, especially thinking that involves the logistics of your novel, the more time you'll free up later in the process for creating, developing, and writing.

At a glance:
Outline Pros: Very detailed—you can add as many layers of detail as you'd like.

Outline Cons: Not as easy to physically manipulate the information once you are writing.

THE SIGNPOST OUTLINE

Those of you who are resistant to the outlining process might find the signpost outline to be of better use. In this kind of outline, you'll fill in "placeholders," which briefly note the kind and type of scene you'll need, the characters and the setting and a general idea of what happens—but not necessarily *all* the details of the scene. (For a more detailed description of scene types, see page 28.) In this type of outline, you'll need to know only the basics, which will still leave plenty of room for you to develop the nuances of the scene while you are writing. Mark Twain used a kind of signpost outline when writing his novel *The Adventures of Tom Sawyer.* That is, he had a general idea of where the novel would go and how the novel would be organized, but the specifics were left until the drafting stage.

For instance, you might know that in one scene your protagonist, Sully, confronts the man he believes to be stalking his wife, Berta. You might know this scene contains a lot of action, a chase, some dialogue toward the end, and the dramatic realization that the stalker is really the biological father of Berta—a man who abandoned her (and her mother) when she was young.

Here is an example of a signpost outline:

SCENE 6: Action scene

SETTING: Sully's backyard and the woods surrounding his property

CHARACTERS: Sully, the Stalker

PLOT: Sully sees the Stalker again, peeking in through the kitchen window to get a glimpse of Berta. Sully grabs his pistol and confronts the man, who runs through the woods. Sully chases him. The man stumbles, and Sully finally catches up. He points the gun at the Stalker and forces him to talk. Dialogue ensues. Man reveals he's Berta's father.

SCENE 7: Contemplative/interior scene

SETTING: The bed-and-breakfast where Berta works as a housekeeper

CHARACTERS: Berta; some guests of the inn; Berta's boss, Larrin

PLOT: Berta goes about her daily task of cleaning the guest rooms, changing linens, scrubbing floors. She contemplates whether she wants to accept her father into her life. She feels loyal to her dead mother, who was betrayed by this man. But he also has money—he's a retired CIA agent and he could finally help provide for Berta and her family. She could quit the job at the inn. As she cleans in this scene and reflects on her dilemma, several guests and even her boss confront her with ridiculous demands, like refilling the Q-tips in Room 22.

SCENE 8: Dialogue scene

SETTING: The rolling park along the river

CHARACTERS: Berta and her father

PLOT: Berta and her father meet for the first time to talk. Berta's father reveals that he left the family because his job was too dangerous (he was, after all, a CIA operative), and he didn't want it to affect those he loved most. Berta is moved by her father's attention, yet she still distrusts him. Aren't CIA agents trained to lie?

The signpost outline is a good choice for you if you're more of a big-picture thinker. This kind of outline gives you a good amount of freedom up front, but it also does not work through all the logistical details of your novel, which means more time connecting the dots during the drafting process.

At a glance:

Outline pros: A good choice for those who scorn the outlining process; allows for a bit more creative discovery during the writing process.

Outline cons: Not as thorough; scenes not as clearly mapped as in some of the other outlining techniques, resulting in potential dead ends.

THE NOTE-CARD TECHNIQUE

Do you remember using flashcards when you were learning something simple back in elementary school, something like the multiplication table or vocabulary words? These cards were an excellent learning tool for many reasons. First, they were portable, so you could take them with you anywhere: to school, to your grandma's house, on the long drive to the beach, to the bathroom. Additionally, you could mix the cards up a bit, shuffle them so you weren't just memorizing the answers in the order of the cards. The inventor of the note card has helped kids through the ages pass math and vocabulary quizzes.

Note cards can be used to outline your novel, too, and offer these similar advantages. When using the note card technique, each individual card is one scene of your novel. You'll name the setting, the characters involved, and the major plot details. You can also list the purpose/goal of the scene.

SETTING: Cruise ship's entertainment deck, Friday night

CHARACTERS: Chet, Dash, Mary Ann, and a Barry Manilow impersonator

- Chet and Dash fight over Mary Ann after she leaves
- Dash breaks a beer bottle on the bar, attempts to stab Chet
- Barry Manilow impersonator, in the middle of his act, sees the fight and comes over to stop it
- Dash accidentally stabs Barry Manilow look-alike.

GOAL: To develop a major plot point that will lead to Mary Ann's crucial decision later in the novel.

The advantage of the note-card technique is that you can easily swap cards around to find the best order for the scenes in your novel. Additionally, it visually breaks the novel into mini compartments, which makes it easy to see how your novel is progressing, how to transition from scene to scene, and what scenes might be missing.

And the best part is they're portable! You can take a stack of note cards to a coffee shop without having to lug your expensive laptop. Just be sure not to spill your latte on them.

At a glance:

Outline pros: Portable; good for those who visually conceptualize novels; easy to change the organization of your novel.

Outline cons: Can be bulky to deal with several scenes at once; no electronic backup, so don't lose them.

THE SPREADSHEET APPROACH

The spreadsheet approach is a bit like an electronic version of the note-card technique. Outlines of this variety are written in a spreadsheet program, such as Microsoft Excel, and allow you to categorize your thoughts, number your scenes, and include whichever kind of information will be helpful to you during the writing process. This is an excellent method because it allows you to insert additional columns, as necessary, which might be particularly useful in week four as you are asked to assess the strength and purpose of each of your individual scenes. It also allows you to easily reorder the columns in only a few clicks, so the information is organized in the way you prefer.

SCENE NUMBER	17
SETTING	Gettysburg Battlefield
CHARACTERS	Buck and Amy
SUMMARY	After hours driving, Buck and Amy arrive to their destination only to be confronted by a major thunderstorm. They park their car by the side of the road and wait. That's when they see it: the newborn baby abandoned beneath the Eternal Light monument. Buck runs out in the storm to get the baby, and Amy swaddles it in her hooded sweatshirt.

SCENE GOAL/ RELATION TO PLOT	Buck and Amy have been trying endlessly to conceive a child, and this is the opportunity they have been waiting for.

The spreadsheet approach will only be useful to you, of course, if you have a decent awareness of how spreadsheets work. If you decide to take this route, yet aren't familiar with the tricks and techniques of a particular program, I suggest you take a brief tutorial, many of which can be found online with a simple Internet search. Learning a program such as Excel is really quite simple, and the ability to quickly sort, organize, or copy/paste information is extremely helpful when drafting your work.

At a glance:

Outline pros: Allows you to manipulate the data as you see fit; helpful when mapping out your novel during the revision process; allows you to easily rearrange and reorganize your novel.

Outline cons: Spreadsheets can be bulky to work with; you'll need to be reasonably familiar with a spreadsheet program for this method to be useful.

THE FLOWCHART

The flowchart is the most tactile of the outlining approaches, and you'll need to have ample space, like an open wall, a bulletin board, or a large whiteboard to adequately employ such a method. A flowchart allows you to more visually envision the progress of your novel in a much less linear way than the other outlining approaches. For instance, you could tack up a note card with the details from one scene (remember, none of these methods will allow for you to get away from developing your individual scenes) and then, using a system of arrows, you can show the fallout from that particular scene for all the characters involved. A flowchart can be confusing for those who are linear thinkers, and such a method can feel a bit antiquated for those of you more accustomed to using your computer to organize your data for you. However, a flowchart allows for a good deal of flexibility when approaching your novel, and it's great for detail-obsessed individuals. Haitian-American writer Edwidge Danticat is known to cut photographs of Haiti out of *National Geographic* and tack it to the board next to her desk to help her with setting and description in her scenes. You can include as much visual information as you want: newspaper clippings, photographs, descriptions, and so on. For instance, if your novel is set near Gettysburg, you'll be able to include photographs that depict the scenery, such as pictures of cannons, memorials, and the battlefield itself.

Example:

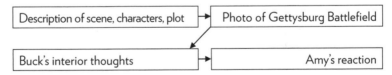

The use of a flowchart is not for everyone, of course—and its uses and potential can vary widely, depending on how visual or tactile a thinker you are. I like it because you can easily add and remove note cards, include sticky notes, and show how different characters move (literally and figuratively) in different directions throughout the novel. However, you'd look a bit strange if you tried to wheel a portable bulletin board into a coffee shop with you, so this kind of outline works best in the privacy of your own home.

At a glance:

Outline pros: Excellent for nonlinear or visual thinkers; allows for a good deal of creativity, even within the outline process; looks impressive to others who might be curious about your progress.

Outline cons: Bulky, nonlinear—sometimes confusing, and a bit archaic.

The above methods are, of course, only suggestions. As you begin experimenting with some or all of them, you may find yourself combining two or more of the methods, e.g. note cards + flowchart, or you may tweak one particular strategy to fit your needs. Remember, this isn't Mrs. N__'s class, and there is no one, correct way to create a working outline. Fantasy writer Marion Zimmer Bradley once noted, "To me, everything in a novel comes down to people making choices. You must figure out in advance what those choices are going to be." Outlining helps you determine what the best choices will be in your novel, so that when it comes time to write your novel, you can simply focus on generating the words, bringing your characters to life, and creating a setting and plot so clearly, so intricately painted that your readers will feel like they are living in the novelistic world you've created for them. The writing is, after all, the fun part. Don't you think?

*W*riting a novel is a bit like cooking a gourmet meal.

You know you must include your individual ingredients: character, plot, setting, conflict, dialogue, action, etc. But how do you know *how* to throw them all together? What balance must you strike to achieve the right flavor?

When you cook a meal, you can't simply walk into the kitchen and magically throw it together. Poof! Voilà! If you've never cooked before, why would you expect the meal to turn out exquisite on your first try? Instead, you must ask yourself, is it better to sauté or bake? Is it better to mince or chop? When should you let the sauce simmer at a low heat versus boil rapidly? Most importantly, you must learn to select ingredients, read recipes, slice, dice, brine, marinate, fold, mix, beat, and broil before you can accomplish the more daunting and difficult tasks of making a soufflé, bouillabaisse, or, that Southern favorite, turducken (a duck stuffed into a chicken stuffed into a turkey).

That is, you must learn a bit more about the parts before you are able to create a whole. You must understand how they come together to achieve that sumptuous balance. Then you're cookin' with Crisco. Or extra-virgin olive oil, for those with more refined palettes.

After spending a good deal of time outlining your novel, you will most likely have a grasp on the discrete elements of your novel: character, tone, voice, setting, dialogue, plot, conflict, etc. However, how will you put all these elements together in order to shape it? How do you draw out character traits and plot conflicts in a convincing and compelling way? How will you balance these elements to achieve novelistic harmony? The first step toward turning your outline into a first draft in ninety days is acknowledging that novels are written scene by scene (by scene by scene, etc.).

THE SCENE DEFINED

Think of your favorite movie. Or better yet, your favorite book. What was your favorite part? Did you say the part in *The Adventures of Tom Sawyer* when Tom returns to hilariously watch his own funeral? How about the part in *The Lovely Bones*, the knockout success by Alice Sebold, when protagonist Susie returns to Earth from Heaven to occupy Ruth's body and finally kiss Ray Singh, the boy she almost loved when alive? How about the part in *Uncle Tom's Cabin* when little Eva—that heavenly angel—passes out locks of her hair before she dies? If you thought of a movie, do you remember the part in the movie *Braveheart* when William Wallace yells, "Freedom!" to a crowd of astonished onlookers? Or how about the part in *Spider-Man* when the masked hero first saves the life of Mary Jane? The two then share that famous upside-down kiss when Mary Jane rolls up half of that mask. (The magic here is that it feels relatively normal—for the viewer—to want Mary Jane to kiss a strange man dressed in a full-body spider suit.)

All these "parts" mentioned above are actually just a single scene from each of these works. But what is a scene?

How does one define it? Scene writing is often difficult to discuss—for both new and seasoned writers—because a scene combines all elements of fiction in harmony with one another. It isn't just one aspect of craft—it's all of them put together, artfully and thoughtfully, to achieve the same kind of balance you hope for in that extravagant dish you prepare for your dinner guests. And how much of any single element (dialogue, setting, description, etc.) you need is going to depend on the particular purpose of the scene within the larger scope of your novel.

Recently, wanting to experiment with a new recipe for saag palak, an Indian dish, I went to my favorite farmer's market to get the ingredients, carefully selecting them one by one. When I got home, I took off my shoes (I like to cook barefoot like my ancestors), and I felt the cool tile on my feet. I began cooking, adding the first main ingredients, spinach and tofu. Once I began adding the spices to the dish, I ran into my first obstacle.

"I'm out of coriander!" I yelled to Rob, who was upstairs watching television.

He popped his head around the corner like a curious squirrel and smiled tentatively. He knew what I was going to ask and volunteered before I got the chance to ask it. "I'll go to the market." This is not the first time this has happened.

When Rob returned, I grabbed the spice jar in haste and, without looking, dumped in about half the contents. I then looked to the recipe I'd printed out. "Too much!" I say, annoyed with myself.

I tried first to remove some of the spice, but I saw it had already seeped into the cooking liquid. Then I compensated by adding more cumin. (This is what anyone in my family does instinctively to remedy mistakes. "Got Cumin?" is a marketing slogan found ... in only one house in America.) But, in this case, cumin was overwhelming the dish, so I added some cinnamon, then some salt, then pepper. When that didn't work, I desperately tried to add other ingredients, cream, more spinach, onion, garlic, yogurt, hot sauce, and even some parsley for good measure, even though the recipe hadn't called for that. I was determined to fix my mistake.

Later that night at dinner, we sat down to the table and took our first bites. Rob looked across the table at me.

"Mmmm," he tried to say but couldn't contain a smile. We both put down our forks, and I somehow managed to swallow the ooey, gooey, ill-textured, sour-tasting glob of muck.

"I'll call for pizza," I said, defeated, but laughing. The universal judgment on this experiment: failure.

This very short story proves just how difficult achieving balance in a meal can be, but it also demonstrates something else: a scene. The story has characters (me, Rob), a conflict (a desperate attempt to fix a ruined meal), setting (my kitchen), interior thoughts (I'm annoyed with myself), action (Rob runs out for spices), character history (my family loves cumin), dialogue ("I'm out of coriander!"), and resolution (pizza). Though I was not able to find the right balance in my saag palak, I was able to achieve balance in the scene itself, and for this I am thankful.

Consider this excerpt of a scene from a more familiar example, the American classic *The Great Gatsby*, which has been labeled [in brackets] to show its discrete scene components:

> I stayed late that night. [Establishes first-person POV] Gatsby asked me to wait until he was free and I lingered in the garden until the inevitable swimming party had run up, chilled and exalted, from the black beach, until the lights were extinguished in the guest rooms overhead. [Description of setting] When he came down the steps at last the

tanned skin was drawn unusually tight on his face, and his eyes were bright and tired. [Character description]

"She didn't like it," he said immediately. [Dialogue]

"Of course she did."   [Dialogue]

"She didn't like it," he insisted. "She didn't have a good time."

He was silent and I guessed at his unutterable depression. [Description of action; Interior or indirect thoughts of narrator; Emotion]

"I feel far away from her," he said. "It's hard to make her understand." [Dialogue that characterizes (Gatsby is sensitive, longs for Daisy); Conflict (Gatsby can't have Daisy)]

"You mean about the dance?" [Dialogue]

"The dance?" He dismissed all the dances he had given with a snap of his fingers. "Old sport, the dance is unimportant." [Dialogue, Emotion]

He wanted nothing less of Daisy than that she should go to Tom and say: "I never loved you." After she had obliterated three years with that sentence they could decide upon the more practical measures to be taken. One of them was that, after she was free, they were to go back to Louisville and be married from her house—just as if it were five years ago. [Emotion; Interior thoughts; Character history]

In this brief snippet of a scene from F. Scott Fitzgerald's seminal novel, the reader learns a great deal in a short space about Gatsby's deep longing for the unattainable Daisy. We learn that he's trying to impress her with his parties; we learn that he's failed; we understand the inherent conflict that presents itself at the core of the novel (unrequited love, a desire to return to the past); we learn that the first-person narrator, Nick Carraway, can often only *guess* at the interior thoughts of the protagonist, Jay Gatsby. And that tells us something, too, about how the novel is narrated to us, the reader. We hear the characters speak, directly from their own mouths; we know a bit about the setting, the plot, and the conflict—and even a bit about the backstory. And all of this, amazingly, in the span of approximately two hundred words! Now that's the epitome of compartmental, and compact, writing—a delicate balancing act in which Fitzgerald juggles several components of fiction. Bravo, Scotty, you master of the novel.

All scenes must work to *do* something in your novel. By that, I mean: All scenes must have a distinct function and purpose within the larger narrative arc of your novel. Think of scenes as the individual bricks that comprise the house of your novel. Or as the single pearls that, strung together, form a beautiful necklace. Or how about the individual notes that combine to create a beautiful melody. Or the days that form the month, or the weeks that shape a year. Or … or … We have an endless store of metaphors at our fingertips. Pick one you like.

Scene writing, however, is where writing your novel can get tricky, as the writer must master the art of gazing outward and downward, a bit like a quarterback, who is constantly looking both at his immediate surroundings, peripherally, so that he doesn't get sacked by the defense, while his eyes are focused downfield for the pass. You, too, must always keep your eyes in two places at once: the micro (the scene) and the macro (the novel). It is essential to constantly consider how each of the "parts" of your novel influences the overall trajectory of your plot and character development.

The poet William Blake unwittingly gives the novelist a bit of advice in his poem "Auguries of Innocence." The poem's first line could be speaking directly about the scene itself: "To see the world in a grain of sand." What Blake means by this is that even something as miniscule as a grain of sand tells us something about the world at large. Or, to put it another way, the part reveals—or at least hints at—the whole. A scene works to accomplish just that; by showing your reader only *part* of the character, the plot, the action, and the development, you are working to reveal a larger, more intricate picture. Consider, for a moment, our example above from *The Great Gatsby*. In this brief excerpt, we can intuit what Gatsby is really like as a character. For one, he's the kind of individual who would use the phrase "old sport," certainly antiquated now, but clearly situating Gatsby in the 1920s era of the novel. We know that Gatsby is hosting a party; yet he cares only for the one opinion that matters most to him: Daisy's. With this scene, this small grain of sand, Fitzgerald provides a glimpse of the entire novel, hinting at both Gatsby's desperation, his romantic nature, his obsessive personality, and, sadly, his ultimate demise.

Another literary master, Ernest "Papa" Hemingway, once famously noted, "If it is any use to know it, I always try to write on the principle of the iceberg. There is seven-eighths of it underwater for every part that shows." What Hemingway is talking about here, of course, is subtext. A well-crafted scene shows the reader only a fraction of what he needs to know, and leaves it up to him or her to intuit the rest. We know that Gatsby is a wealthy, 1920s-era fellow because he uses the phrase "old sport." Fitzgerald didn't need to tell us this directly. "Old sport" is also a term of endearment that reveals Gatsby's affection for his young friend Nick. How might Gatsby have been perceived if he called Nick "old buddy, old pal" or "bud" or "Nicky"? In that case, Gatsby certainly wouldn't be Gatsby, now, would he?

I encourage you to think of each individual scene as an opportunity to reveal to your reader some new aspect of your character or your plot. So, for instance, if in one scene of *The Great Gatsby* we learn of Jay Gatsby's lavish, though vacuous, parties, his fancy shirts, and his ornately decorated bachelor pad, in another chapter we may learn that he cares little for these things, instead devoting his emotions fully to Daisy, the one possession his money can't buy.

With each scene you write, you should be able to answer the following questions:

- What is the goal/purpose for the scene?
- What characters are involved in this scene, and are they all necessary?
- What is at stake for my protagonist in this scene?
- What is the main conflict in this scene?
- How does this scene further develop my novel's plot?

(Note: You should be able to answer these questions even before you've actually written the scene, as we'll be doing in the following weeks. However, thinking about the purpose of the scene in the initial weeks will save you the task of cutting scenes that aren't "doing the necessary work" in your novel. This will, in turn, save you valuable days during your ninety-day challenge.)

If, as you peruse your outline at the end of the first four weeks, you're unable to come up with a clear intention of a given scene, you might be wiser to cut that scene or redirect it. Perhaps the conflict is not deep enough. How can you further develop the character and his history? How can you beef up this scene so it's not just empty calories in the meal that is your novel?

SCENE STRUCTURE

We'll discuss the structure of your whole novel at length in a later section of this book, but if you recall anything from your high school English classes, those long days when you diagrammed the structure of a novel, you probably remember the simple fact that novels have a beginning, a middle, and an end. (This is often diagrammed to look like an inverted V or the tip of a mountain or an A without the middle connector. You get the point.) All stories and novels have rising action, a climax, and falling action, resulting in a resolution. Characters and plots are introduced, tensions rise, conflicts are confronted, and choices are made, which result in the outcome of the story's end, be it happy or sad.

Here's something you may not have considered, however: Individual scenes, too, must have a beginning, a middle, and an end. It's a simple lesson, but one worth discussing in advance of any scene writing so your scenes feel like finished snapshots and not half-developed Polaroid pictures. It's an easy and common mistake to create a scene that hasn't been fully developed—that has no clear ending, no discernable middle, or a hastily scrawled start. In other words, a scene that has no point. These types of scenes often leave readers scratching their heads, wondering, "What am I supposed to do with *that?*"

Scenes are mini modules, a single unit of your novel. However, each unit must still stand as a cohesive whole. That is, if you took each scene out of your novel, it should be able to stand alone—perhaps not as complete as a story itself, but as a mini story that leaves your reader feeling like they've learned something about the characters involved or about the unraveling plot. Did the scene above from *The Great Gatsby* reveal anything new or interesting about the characters? Did the scene help forward the plot? The answers are yes and yes. This snapshot emphasizes Gatsby's unalterable fixation on Daisy. Everything he does, he does for her. Everything. Including, one might add, moving to West Egg, setting up house across the lake from the green light of Daisy's dock, and throwing lavish parties to impress her. What else might he do in the name of this obsessive love? Keep reading and find out, the novel suggests.

Beginnings, middles, and endings each hold a particular function within the scene. It's important to recognize the importance of scene structure before penning a single word of your novel.

The Beginning of a Scene

You should aim to begin a majority of your scenes in *medias res*, or, in the middle of the action. When a reader starts reading a scene, she should feel *already* immersed in the action—she should feel as though she has to keep reading in order to catch up with the plot that is evolving before her eyes. Though you may choose to begin some scenes with description of the setting or, perhaps, the philosophical musing of the narrator, you should introduce your character by the second or third paragraph of each scene—otherwise you risk losing the interest of your reader. Yes, the Red Rocks of Arizona might be beautiful—I know, I've been there!—but your reader will find the beauty only lackluster without the necessary characters to populate the scene. Have you ever had a friend share with you his photos from a vacation he had taken? You might remember, then, how you had to feign interest as he showed you photo after photo after photo of the landscapes, the foliage, the wildlife, the flowers. Where are you in these pictures, you might ask him. Good question.

A scene without characters is not really a scene at all. Engage the interest of your reader by connecting them immediately to your characters. People, quite simply, are very interested in reading about other people.

The Middle of a Scene

All characters must want something within an individual scene, and in your scene middle you must complicate the attainment of this "something." What is standing in the way of what your character wants? Scene middles are the territory of conflict.

Fiction writer Anne Lamott wrote, "You are going to love some of your characters, because they are you or some facet of you, and you are going to hate some of your characters for the same reason. But no matter what, you are probably going to have to let bad things happen to some of the characters you love or you won't have much of a story. Bad things happen to good characters, because our actions have consequences, and we do not behave perfectly all the time." Simply stated, scene middles are the place for bad things to happen to your characters—for something to get in the way of what they want, for conflict to arise, and for them to face this conflict and respond to it in a way that is emblematic of their character. In some scenes this conflict will be obvious (e.g., "I need to get to the other side of the cliff, but the bridge is broken") and in other scenes, the conflict will be more subtle, (e.g., "I'm going to my high school reunion and I'm nervous to see my ex, who doesn't know I'm divorced"). Whether your conflict is large or small, the scene middle is where your character confronts and reacts. This process of acting and reacting is what will propel your scene, and therefore your plot, forward.

The End of a Scene

The ending for each scene need not be a definitive ending, unless it's one of the final scenes of your novel. You may choose to end some scenes with a plot cliff-hanger, an unspoken "To be continued ..." clause that encourages your reader to keep turning the page. Or, perhaps, like a filmmaker, you might zoom in to the character's head as he contemplates the events that have just unfolded before him. Conversely, you may choose to end by focusing on a particularly symbolic metaphor. As you zoom out of the scene, perhaps the silhouette of a bird flies away in the distance, which might allude to the loneliness of your protagonist. Think of scene endings as "breathers" for your reader—a paragraph or two that allows him to take in and process, along with your characters, what just happened in the scene.

But here's a caveat: Unless you know the purpose or goal of your scene, you may not know how to end it properly. If you, the writer, don't clearly understand the intention of your scene, you can confidently bet your reader won't either. Readers don't like to guess at the point of a scene, nor should they have to—and there's a clear difference between not giving away too much in one scene and being downright ambiguous. Be sure you can distinguish between the two.

SCENE VARIETY

Scene writing will be fundamental to developing and drafting your novel, and the more attention you pay during the drafting stages to establishing strong, complete scenes that have a specific purpose within your novel, the less time you'll have to spend later with your old pal, the delete key. But it's also important to identify the various types of scenes that will be useful to you as you work through your novel.

Perhaps it seems obvious, but no two scenes can accomplish the same task in exactly the same way. Unless you want to bore your reader, you'll need to vary the types of scenes you use. For instance, in one scene, your plot might need to be forwarded with a dramatic action; another scene might be needed to show the interiority of your protagonist. Yet another scene might be needed to show characters interacting and discussing events in their own words; you'll also need to include a scene or two revealing the emotional core of your character—or to cast the drama in a different light. Other scenes might use the setting to reveal the tone or mood of your character.

We will explore these types of scenes as we continue throughout the ninety-day challenge, but for now, I'd like to categorize these scenes as *internal* and *external* scenes. Of course, these are somewhat fluid, overlapping categories, but for the sake of definition, internal scenes are primarily focused on what is going on inside your character's head, whereas in external scenes your characters are engaging with the world at large. There can be an internal portion of an external scene, or vice versa. However, a primary internal scene works to reveal an aspect of character while a primary external scene works to unravel an element of plot.

Internal Scenes

Much of our life happens in our heads. Today, for instance, I went to the grocery store, and as I walked by the spice aisle I sneezed (the pepper, no doubt), which reminded me of an article I read about how blueberries are a superfood, which sent me down the organic section looking for blueberries. But before I got there, I knocked my cart into a cereal display, which sent the pyramid of boxes crashing to the floor. I was so mad at myself. *Stupid, stupid, stupid,* I was thinking. The employee who kindly reset the display resembled a younger version of this boy I once dated in college. I wondered what he is doing now. He was always good at science.

To my loved ones at the end of the day, I might simply report: I went to the grocery store. My day involved much more complexity than that, however. My internal world was a veritable roller coaster. I bet yours was, too, if you consider the thoughts inside your head. I just made you think this thought inside your head, by the way. Gotcha. And I don't even know you. See how a bit of internal thinking can work? Powerful stuff.

All novels need glimpses into the character's internal worlds. Without these hints at a character's thoughts and emotions, novel reading would be about as passionate as kissing the Blarney Stone.

Setting: Contemplative Scenes

In these scenes, setting becomes almost a character itself, reflecting the mood, values, and mind-set of your character. For instance, if your character feels empty, numb, or emotionless, a desert setting might be used to convey these thoughts. When a person feels in good spirits, he sees blue skies, hears chirping birds, and feels a refreshing cool breeze on his skin. When a person is in a bad mood, he'll likely notice negative things: carpet stains, cracks in the gray sidewalk, crumbling brick buildings.

Emotional Scenes

Emotional scenes do just what you think they do: reveal a character's emotions. Here's a general rule for dealing with emotions in fiction: Never explicitly state the emotion. Do not write, "He was sad" or "He felt happy." I'm sure you've heard the rule: Show, don't tell. Readers do not like to be told how they're supposed to read a scene. Instead, readers relate to emotions through physical sensations. If you use an emotional scene to reveal Kevin's anger at having learned his bar, Milton's, was robbed, don't write: "Kevin was mad." Instead, show it: "Kevin's hands balled up into fists that turned red and then white. His face felt hot, like a tea kettle about to explode with steam. He bit the inside of his cheek and tasted blood, warm and metallic...."

Indirect Thought/Interior Monologue Scenes

A good way to know what your character is thinking is to simply let your reader inside your character's head. This becomes especially interesting and useful when what your character thinks is different than how your character acts (or what he says directly). Let your character ramble a little bit—it's a novel, you've got some wiggle room—but be sure that her ramblings are related to the plot of the novel. That is, it's more useful to "hear" Sally reflect on her husband's affair with the deli girl than it is to hear Sally pontificate about how she hates to wear panty hose. (That is, unless the restrictiveness of control-top panty hose is in some ways a metaphor for her restrictive relationship with her husband. Or her longing for Spanx reveals self-image problems that foreshadow later issues with Twinkies.)

External Scenes

One of the biggest mistakes of first-time novel writers (and second-, third-, and fourth-time novel writers, too) is creating a novel that is entirely *too* internal. That is, writers often develop intriguing and complex characters, yet fail to engage them with other characters in their fictional worlds. Boredom is the result.

Stop reading for a moment and make a quick list of all the people you've come into contact with today. Your list might look something like this:

Coffee-shop barista
Newspaper-stand guy
Doorman at office building
Various coworkers
Manicurist
Doctor
People at bus stop
Other patrons of the bar
Little old lady who dropped her grocery bag

Every day, you come into contact with dozens of people, if you're not a hermit, and some of these meetings and connections are more significant than others. Your protagonist, too, should interact with the world at large. Not all the "contacts" you've listed are major players in your life, but even minor characters can reveal something about you as an individual. (Charles Dickens famously populated his novels with dozens of characters, some fairly insignificant, but fun to meet.) For instance, when the little old lady dropped her groceries, did you walk on by or did you stop and help her pick up her scattered goods? The takeaway point is this: You need to allow your characters to engage with a cast of characters, for each interaction gives your readers another piece of your novel's puzzle. Good novels thrive on a diverse and varied ensemble. In external scenes, characters confront characters.

Dialogue Scenes

Allowing your character to speak—in her own words—is vital to your novel. We learn a lot about a character when she talks. First, *how* does she talk? Does she have a lilt to her voice? A Southern drawl? A New Jersey accent? Does she use an elevated vocabulary: "I love the anthropomorphism of a character such as Bambi." Or does she speak in short, choppy sentences: "It's weird that Bambi is a talking deer." These details will all help crystallize your character in the mind of your reader. Consider, too, when *what* a character says differs from what he thinks. Have you ever given a false compliment? "I just loved looking at all your landscape photos from your recent vacation out West! Who needs *people* in their pictures anyway?" you might have told your friend, while in truth you were bored out of your gourd. Scenes involving large portions of dialogue, if done well, can draw out conflict, reveal tensions, and unearth hidden sentiments. Another benefit of a dialogue scene is that it can quicken the pace of your novel and keep the reader turning pages. What will they say next?

Action Scenes

These scenes narrate plot-forwarding action, and the pacing of these scenes, like the action itself, should be quick. As such, it's important to begin these scenes in *medias res* in order to get the reader immediately hooked by the action. Be sure to use as many sensory details as possible in these types of scenes: What does your character see, hear, smell, feel? And, to be clear, don't be totally fooled by the term *action* scene. An action scene is just as much about the action or plot point itself as it is about the *reaction* of the character to the events that are unfolding before them. Sometimes it's best to let your characters act first, then think later. F. Scott Fitzgerald said it best: "There is no 'safety first' in Art!" Having your characters deal with the fallout as it occurs is a good way to build tension in your work because they'll have to deal with consequences later.

Dramatic scenes

Creating drama—though not melodrama!—is important to any work of fiction. Dramatic scenes are like action scenes; however, the pacing is a bit slower, and the focus is a bit more internal. An example of a dramatic scene in *The Great Gatsby* might be when Tom Buchanan drives by the scene of his lover's accident. Tom quickly hops out of his car and learns, or believes, that Gatsby has hit and killed Myrtle going sixty miles an hour, never stopping. The reader understands, in this moment, Tom's emotional connection to Myrtle and his deep hatred for Gatsby: Tears roll down his face as he leaves the gruesome scene, cursing Gatsby as a coward. Dramatic scenes precariously balance action, discovery, and emotion. And they can add tantalizing bits of conflict for later consumption.

Now that we've reviewed some of the fundamentals of outlines and scene writing, buckle your seatbelt, set your start date, sign your contract, and get ready to do some writing. The first day of your novel writing challenge starts as soon as you're ready.

Part 2:

THE 90-DAY WRITING CHALLENGE

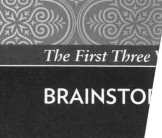
Each day during thes
duced to a specific co
be asked to comple
designed to add
assignment w
some of y
the first
inten
of

Have you ever
This is a good ...
of your ninety-day writing challeng
you'll be brainstorming, developing, and scrutinizing
details of your novel—characters, plots, conflicts, settings,
voice, point of view, etc.—and, eventually, you'll draft your
initial working outline, the blueprint of your novel itself.
Think of these first four weeks as your apprenticeship for
the novel-writing process that will follow.

Great novels are not accidents. As much as you want
to believe they are simply spawned from the brains of
the greatest creative thinkers, in actuality, they take careful planning, developing, trimming, shaping, and forecast-
ing. By now, hopefully you realize the necessity of an outline in an undertaking such as this one. And though you
may be tempted to simply skip ahead and begin writing
your novel's first draft, I caution you against it. You first
want to make sure your ideas are solid, your characters
are complex, and your plots are sustainable. If you do the
necessary work in the planning stages, you'll leave little to
chance when you sit down to write your novel. Remember,
our first ideas are not always our best ideas.

first three weeks you'll be intro-
ponent of novel writing, and you'll
e an assignment. These assignments are
ess key elements of your novel, and each
ll build upon the next. You may end up using
ur assignments from these weeks verbatim in
draft of your novel. Other assignments are simply
ed to help you develop and flesh out the direction
your ideas and will not be used directly—though likely
indirectly—in your work.

You should plan on spending about thirty minutes reading and thinking about each day's lesson and at least an
additional two to three hours per day working on the writing exercises. Remember, the more work you do in the
developmental stages now, the more you'll be freed up to
creatively explore your novelistic world during the drafting stages. You'll find no easy shortcuts, so be sure to allot
yourself an adequate amount of time as you approach each
day's assignments.

EIGHT SUGGESTIONS BEFORE YOU START:

1. Buy a timer and place it next to you as you write. This
   will help you keep track of how long you've been working—and how much time you have to go.
2. Place a "Do Not Disturb" note on your office door
   when you're writing, if you don't live alone.
3. Turn your phone to silent and don't check it—or better
   yet, turn it off.
4. If you work on a computer, log off from the Internet.
   This way you won't be tempted to check your e-mail or
   procrastinate by checking the weather.

90 DAYS TO YOUR NOVEL

5. Try to write at the same time every day, if possible. Doing so will help you foster a good writing habit.

6. Avoid too much television watching during the next few months. Instead, read some novels. Good ideas are often generated from reading and are seldom generated from Must-See TV.

7. Use the buddy system. If you know a friend, a group of friends, or even a writing group comprised of individuals who want to write a novel, take the ninety-day challenge together. You can reinforce each other, commiserate, inspire, complain, and help each other over those difficult writing slumps. Writing is a solitary enterprise, but talking about writing isn't.

8. Have fun! You're about to take those first teetering, yet exhilarating steps toward writing your novel. Embrace the challenge.

DAY 1: *Ready, Set, Go (With What You Know)*

You've always wanted to write a novel, but perhaps you don't even know where to begin brainstorming sustainable, book-length-worthy plots and characters. If you're like me, you may make mental notes to yourself throughout the week: "That'd be a good idea for a novel." However, when it comes time to sit at my writing desk, I've forgotten some of my best ideas (unless I've written them down). They've disappeared into the ether of my brain, likely replaced by a grocery list or an errand I have to run. The good news is this: Ideas for your novel are all around you—within you, too. In fact, you may already know some of the characters or settings you'll be writing about. You just don't know it yet.

You've probably heard the old writer's dictum, "Write what you know." This, of course, is excellent advice; however, it does not simply mean you should only write about, literally, the people and places with which you have direct contact and intimate familiarity. Not only could that get really tiresome really quickly, but it might be better saved for your memoir or personal biography. However, your experiences and memories—the fine, rich details that form the tapestry of your life—make for excellent novelistic fodder and are often fantastic jumping points for exploring fictional worlds.

Meditating on your earliest childhood memories might trigger some noteworthy visual pictures: that concrete culvert you and your neighbors used to pretend was a bunker; a spot in the woods where a willow tree drooped its branches, creating a perfect imaginary house; the basement of the McDowells' house that was lined from ceiling to floor with a collection of eclectic beer cans; or Janis Putts, your old neighbor who exiled you from her yard for stepping in her petunias. (You were only four, and that's where your ball landed!)

Reaching back into the crevices of your brain, you might find some interesting and noteworthy characters, too. Individuals who were minor players in your real life, might somehow find their way onto the stage in the starring role in your novel's world: Just who was that old man who was always sitting with a suitcase at the bus stop on Fifth Street? And why did Mrs. Ortenwagner live alone in that huge house up the hill? She would always retrieve the mail in her housecoat and slippers, her hair rolled up in curlers, even though she never seemed to go anywhere. Why did Miguel Mylar, the science teacher, burst into tears that day back in high school? He never came back to McKnight High after that. I've always wondered....

Memory can provide us with rich and intricate details that we might not even realize we remembered. What was your first memory? What did it feel like to be kissed the first time? What were some of your favorite smells as a child—and now as an adult? What was the most daring thing you ever did, or *wished* you did? Did you ever come close to getting everything you've ever wanted? Have you ever read a news story that just stuck with you because it was so bizarre, grotesque, or surreal? Have you ever seen a sight you wished you hadn't seen?

When we explore our memories, we are not simply transporting ourselves back to the past, but we're using our memories and imaginations to embellish what we once thought we knew. Philip Roth once explained, "Obviously the facts are never just coming at you but are incorporated by an imagination that is formed by your previous experience. Memories of the past are not memories of facts but memories of your imaginings of the facts." What Roth means is that memories aren't the literal events as they happened, but events as we always imagined they happened, in our minds. At their core, then, memories are embellished stories dissimilar from the original thing itself. Exploring your own history will help you embellish, expand, and manipulate experiences into fictional elements that resemble nothing of the original memory itself.

Assignment

In this exercise, brainstorm as many early memories as you can, writing them out in as much detail as possible, dedicating at least a paragraph to each. For this exercise, do not worry about writing in scene or editing yourself as you go. The goal is to keep brainstorming and to keep writing, as much as possible in the minimum of two hours you're allotting yourself. If this is the first time you've written in a while, don't feel pressured to write something perfect. Just let yourself write freely as you think about each memory. I've provided some prompts to get you started, though please don't feel limited to these categories.

PEOPLE: Your favorite or worst teacher, the postman, your first babysitter, your neighbors, your first boyfriend/girlfriend, your childhood best friend, someone who got you in trouble, someone you admired from a distance, someone you thought was beautiful, your grandparents or most distant relative, the saddest person you ever saw, somebody you knew by sight but never met in person.

PLACES: The inside of your house, your bedroom, your favorite place to play as a child, somewhere you go when you want to be alone, your favorite vacation spot, the most cheerful place you ever visited, the most frightening place you've ever been. Perhaps a place you weren't supposed to be?

THINGS: Your favorite coat as a child, your prized childhood possession, the way someone close to you smelled, your first pet, an old photograph that sticks out in your mind, the purse your mother used to carry, the sounds outside your window, how you felt when you gave/received your first kiss, how you felt at a time when you knew you did something wrong, how you felt when you didn't get the praise you deserved.

DAY 2: *Writing With Your Senses*

Yesterday you spent some time recalling your own memories. As you brainstormed, hopefully you came up with some seedlings of an idea that, with planting, nurturing, and a little patience, might bloom into your novel. But even the greatest ideas in the world won't take off if the writing falls flat. Or, to think of it another way, a rather bland idea can blossom if conveyed in a compelling way, through nurturing, life-giving details.

Every writer aims to immerse the reader so deeply into the story, to so hypnotize the reader with the details and the writing, that she continues turning the pages. You want your reader to feel like she's literally present in your fictional world, running right alongside your characters as they get swept up in the action of the story. This is, after all, one of the reasons people read: to lose themselves in a world more interesting than their own.

Remember: Show, don't tell. This old writer's adage asks that writers not simply "report" the story: A man walked down the street. Instead, you should show us the man: Who is the man? What does he look like? How old is he? You should clarify his actions: How is he walking? Quickly or slowly? Does he limp? Are his shoulders hunched? You should show us the street: Is it urban or suburban? Wide or narrow? Is there a sidewalk? Is it littered? And, above all, you should give a reason for his walking: Is his car broken down? Is he on his way to work? Does he plan to meet someone soon? Or is this walk merely for exercise? Will he break into a run? All these details, put together, will create a much more cohesive and fully alive snapshot of the man walking down the street.

The best way to connect a reader to your story is through the senses. Consider this brief example from Flannery O'Connor's short story "The Life You Save May Be Your Own":

> The old woman didn't change her position until he was almost in her yard; then she rose with one hand fisted on her hip. The daughter, a large girl in a blue organdy dress, saw him all at once and jumped up and began to stamp and point and make excited speechless sounds.

In this snippet from O'Connor, a master of the short story, the reader can both see and hear the characters. We're given colors (a blue organdy dress), motions (a fisted hand), and noises (excited speechless sounds) that help this scene materialize for the reader. Likewise, you should always offer your reader concrete and specific detail and use the senses as a guide. What can your characters taste, smell, see, feel, and hear? If you want your reader immersed in the story, they'll need to taste, smell, see, feel, and hear these things, too.

Another lesson for making your story leap off the page will bring us back to high school English class. Do you remember studying active versus passive voice? Hurry, pop quiz:

Which of the following sentences is in active voice?

> Julie is loved by David.

> David loves Julie.

How about this one?

> I heard from my sister that Shelby was accepted to a prestigious clown school.

> It was heard by me from my sister that Shelby was accepted to a prestigious clown school.

Here's another:

The award for Student of the Year was won by Laura.

Laura won the award for Student of the Year.

Extra credit: Do you remember the definition of active voice? Answer: In the active voice, the subject of the sentence is doing the action. In passive voice, the subject of the sentence is receiving the action. One surefire way to recognize passive voice in your writing, and then subsequently eliminate it, is to find and replace many of the "be" verbs with sharper, stronger verbs. Another pop quiz: What are the "be" verbs? These, of course, are all the forms of the verb "to be."

am
is
are
was
were
being
been

So what does this grammar lesson have to do with writing a novel? Simply this: Writing in active voice makes writing more vivid, convincing, and confident. Active voice also helps you avoid unnecessary redundancy and awkward phrasings because active voice is more direct. Passive voice tends to lead to generalizations, and sentences or descriptions that lack specificity.

This is not to say that passive voice has no place in your fiction, and certainly it's not realistic—or possible—to eliminate all uses of passive voice. However, good fiction writers pay attention to the difference between active and passive voice and, when they can, strive for the former rather than the latter.

But who wants to talk about grammar issues? Not me, other than to say this: The goal of your grammar usage in your novel is simple: Aim for invisibility. If your reader notices your usage, or rather, your *incorrect* usage, of grammar, punctuation, or other typos in your text, you're going to draw them out of your story and onto the physical page. They'll remember that they're reading, not skiing in Aspen or investigating the black market in human organs with the characters you've created. If you do not know the general rules of grammar, you should look them up. Sooner rather than later. Like now. Consider purchasing a book such as the short, influential text *The Elements of Style* by Strunk and White.

Assignment

The goal of this assignment is to practice writing with your senses. Select two memories from yesterday's writing and write a scene bringing each of these memories to life. What do you remember seeing, hearing, smelling, tasting, feeling, or thinking? Try to provide as many details as possible, as you reimagine the event in your mind. How can you make the story come alive for your readers?

Next, I want you to print out and reread through what you've just written. Any time you come across one of the "be" verbs, I want you to circle it. Do you find yourself using these verbs often? Have you tried, whenever possible, to be aware of the active voice in your work?

DAY 3: *Letting Your Old Ladies Scream*

Think, for a moment, of your favorite novel—what is it you like about it? Even if you read it long ago, what do you remember? Chances are, you remember Bridget Jones's hilarious self-deprecation in *Bridget Jones's Diary*, or the forever angst-ridden and jaded Holden Caulfield in *The Catcher in the Rye*. Even if you've forgotten the plot, you'll likely remember the commonsense ingenuity of Tom Sawyer, the idealism and naive romanticism of Emma Bovary, or the vapid party guests of the money-and-love-obsessed Jay Gatsby.

The characters you cast for your novel will be the single most important factor in your book. Why? Because characters are the driving force of your novel, the lifeblood of fiction, and nearly every other element of your novel is related to the characters you choose. For example, what happens to your characters and how they respond is your plot. Style and tone and voice reflect your character's intellect, personality, and mood. Even setting is determined in large part by your character. Where does he or she choose to live? What do her home and surroundings say about her? Does her bedroom have black lights and psychedelic posters or ornately framed original artwork and a bowl of cinnamon potpourri? These decisions are reflective of character, too.

Mark Twain explains to us, "Don't tell us that the old lady screamed. Bring her on and let her scream." Twain reminds us that when we create characters so complete, so fully rounded, they'll jump off the page and feel so real that the reader just *knows* them. The reader can actually hear, in their minds, your old ladies screaming; they aren't simply told that the old ladies are hollering. That makes for a big difference in the reading experience.

When we use the phrase "She is such a character!" typically, we mean that the personality of that individual—let's name her Glenda—is so particular *to Glenda* that nobody else is quite like her. Maybe she's exceptionally daffy or neat to a fault. Maybe she asks you to put plastic baggies around your feet as you walk through her house. ("Common household dust is the number-one cause of asthma in cats!" she might say. Oh, dear. That's *so* Glenda.)

Let's return, for a moment, to Ernest Hemingway's theory of the iceberg that we explored in a previous section. Hemingway once wrote, "If a writer of prose knows enough about what he is writing about he may omit things that he knows, and the reader, if the writer is writing truly enough, will have a feeling of those things as strongly as though the writer had stated them. The dignity of movement of the iceberg is due to only one-eighth of it being above water. The writer who omits things because he does not know them only makes hollow places in his writing." Hemingway's theory of the iceberg is quite similar to William Blake's grain of sand. If we know our characters—and I mean *really* know our characters—our readers will, by default, feel they truly know them, too. We don't have to be told that Huck Finn would rather wear overalls than dress pants—we've been given one-eighth a glimpse of him, and we can figure out the rest for ourselves.

But how well do you need to know your character before you begin? We'll be discussing character development in depth later in this book, but before you even write a single word, you should consider all aspects of your character's history, experiences, baggage, complications, fears, and desires. But in addition to these "big" aspects of character, you should also know some smaller, finer nuances. For instance, do you know their favorite flavors of ice cream? How about their shoe sizes? If they were going to buy a pair of shoes, what brand would they most likely purchase? Gucci or Birkenstocks? Hiking boots or stilettos?

We can *guess* that Jay Gatsby's favorite flavor of ice cream is double-chocolate chip—as rich and decadent as you can get. We might guess that, if he were still alive, he'd buy only the most expensive suits from Brooks Brothers. His bedroom might be deep mahogany because it *feels* rich. Even though F. Scott Fitzgerald never mentions these details in his novel, he showed us one-eighth of the iceberg, and we were able to intuit—subtextually—the other seven-eighths.

Here are some other, less obvious questions you might want to consider:

- What does your character want most in life?
- What was the most important thing to have ever happened to your character?
- What is this character's middle name?
- Where does your character work?
- What is this character's favorite thing about himself?
- How does this character drink her coffee?
- What is this character's favorite holiday?
- What kind of music might this character listen to?
- What is the color of this character's bedroom?
- What are this character's favorite childhood memories?
- What age was this character when he first kissed a girl? What was her name?
- What scares this character the most?

At this point, as you begin to brainstorm a cast of characters, you don't necessarily need to know what your character will "do" in your novel, or what role he or she will play. You simply need to know enough about your character so that when faced with a difficult or character-defining decision in your novel, you won't have to wonder how he or she will react. Like muscle memory, your character's natural personality traits and desires will determine these decisions for you.

Assignment

The goal of this assignment is to familiarize yourself with a minimum of ten characters. First, select three "people" you revisited in your Day 1 exercise and write a one-page character bio for each. You'll want to consider not only your character's history, experiences, family, and outlook, but also some of the smaller details listed in the questions above. (See sample Character Bio Worksheet on page 61; I encourage you to make copies and use this as a template for your work.)

Once you've completed these three character bios, write a character bio for at least seven other interesting or compelling characters that may become a part of your novel. Remember: Don't worry at this point about each character's actual role in your novel. Simply focus on getting to know your characters the best you can.

I suggest posting these bios to the bulletin board above your desk, or putting them all in a three-ringed binder and referring back to them later in the writing process, when you're questioning what your character would do in a particular situation.

CHARACTER BIO WORKSHEET

Character name: ....

Age: ....

Occupation:..

Family members and/or significant others: ....
....

Personality traits:..
....

Character history (where is he/she from): ....
....

Highest Level of education: ....

Physical traits:...
....

Biggest motivator: ....
....

Biggest fear: ....
....

Things he/she likes:..
....

Things he/she dislikes: ....
....

Where does he/she live? ....

What kind of music does he/she listen to? ....
....

What does he/she like about him/herself? ....

What does he/she dislike about him/herself? ....

What is his/her favorite childhood memory? ....
....

What is his/her most traumatic life event? ....
....

What is his/her most prized possession? ....

What kind of transportation does he/she use? ....

What is his/her favorite food? ....

What is the most interesting thing about this character? ....
....

What does this character's voice sound like? ....
....

If limited to five words, which ones would most people who know this character use to describe him/her? ....
....

Fiction writer Flannery O'Connor wrote, "If nothing happens, it's not a story." In a story, something happens. Sounds pretty simple, right? In your story something has to happen, and we often refer to this as your plot.

We spent some time talking about character in the previous lessons because character is absolutely crucial to all novel writing, whether you're writing a character-based novel or a plot-based novel. On some levels these distinctions are meaningless: characters are absolutely central to both types of novels.

It's less useful to think about plot as *what happens* in a novel. Instead, it's more useful to think about it as *what happens to a particular character and how she responds to it, thus causing other plot points.* Flannery O'Connor might have said, "If nothing happens to *someone,* it's not a story." In a story, something happens to *someone.* And depending on your character's motivations and desires, his fears and values, just *how* he responds to this "something" will differ. For example, a lawyer will respond differently to witnessing a car accident than a doctor would. The lawyer might be primarily concerned with assessing fault, while the doctor first checks to see if everyone is okay.

Fiction writer and critic E.M. Forster, in his book *Aspects of the Novel,* defines plot's function with the novel as being causal in nature. That is, one event causes another, and this is how plot differs from its more chronological cousin *story.* The example he gives us is simple: "The king died and then the queen died" is not a plot. Instead, this is simply a listing of events that happened, perhaps chronologically, without a cause-and-effect relationship. "The king died and then the queen died of grief"—now this, says Forster, is a plot. The king dies, for whatever reason (in our example let's say the king is goodly and kind, so let's imagine the reasons were quite natural, old age, perhaps), and then the queen becomes grief-stricken. Perhaps she won't eat or sleep. Perhaps this exacerbates an underlying condition. The king died, and the queen responded with grief, thus dying herself. But Forster's example could have continued: What happens next, after the queen dies? Perhaps the kingdom is inherited by the royal couple's greedy, short, balding son, who feels quite self-conscious about his shiny globe. He forces all his subjects to shave their heads—but one person resists. What happens next? Well, depending on the characters' motivations and personality, the plot will evolve accordingly. Will the town become shaven ditto heads, or will one man lead a coiffure mutiny?

Plot is not simply an arbitrary decision made by you, the writer. Instead, the plot derives from the natural reactions of your characters to the events that unfold throughout the novel. If the queen hadn't loved the king, for instance, borrowing again from E.M. Forster's example, she may have lived a long life, quickly taking another husband. Certainly this would have changed the outcome of the unfolding plot. The more you know your characters before you begin writing your novel, the more natural the responses will seem to your reader. You'll have an easier time writing your scenes, too, if you have a sense of how a character, based on his or her personality, might react in a given situation.

While there is no magic formula that generates page-turning plots, consider this quotation from fiction writer Robert Olen Butler: "Fiction is the art form of human yearning. That is absolutely essential to any work of fictional narrative art—a character who yearns. And that is not the same as a character who simply has problems.... The yearning is also the thing that generates what we call plot, because the elements of the plot come from thwarted or blocked or challenged attempts to fulfill the yearning."

Simply put: Yearning generates plot.

Your characters must want something—must yearn for something—and if you wish to sustain your novel's plot, you, the writer, must not give it to him. You should ask yourself these questions:

- What does my character want most in the world?
- What obstacles, events, or people will stand in the way of my character getting what he wants?

Gatsby, more than money, parties, and fancy shirts, wants Daisy. What's standing in his way? Well, Daisy's husband, Tom Buchanan, for one. It is this profound longing that propels the major plot points in *The Great Gatsby*. Gatsby both acts and reacts to his yearning and his thwarted desires.

Assignment

First, for a warm-up: From the chart on page 66, choose a character from list A, and a quality from list B, and write a one-hundred–word character sketch. Next, choose a situation from list C. Brainstorm the ways in which such a character, when faced with this particular situation, might naturally react to or against it. The purpose of this exercise is to demonstrate that plot isn't simply what happens, but rather how a character responds to a given situation. Write a short scene. (You may find that you like your character in this exercise, and if so, feel free to write up a longer character bio to include in your binder.)

LIST A	LIST B	LIST C
A celebrity chef	Sinister	Gets in a car accident
An Elvis impersonator	Alcoholic	Wins the lottery
A failed Wall Street broker	Sexist	Accidentally kills a man
A social climber	Anxious	Enters hot-dog-eating contest
A lottery winner	Narcoleptic	Finds self in bank holdup
A Civil War reenactor	Egomaniacal	Finds baby on doorstep
A movie extra	Hyper-self-conscious	Goes to high school reunion
A Political Activist	Germaphobe	Sets a house on fire

Because this is the first scene you're writing in this process, it's good to remind yourself that all scenes have a beginning, a middle, and an end. Can you recognize each of these parts in your scenes?

Now, I'd like you to spend some time with at least five characters you wrote bios for on Day 2. For each character, write a paragraph answering the following questions: What does my character want most in the world? What obstacles, events, or people will stand in the way of my character getting what he wants? This may take you some time because you'll need to reread the bios and refamiliarize yourself with the personality traits, history, and life experiences of each one.

Once you have finished, you'll have a greater sense of what motivates your characters and what, in turn, will propel your novel forward. But you're not done writing for the day! Before you take off your writer's cap, I want you to compose a 250-word synopsis for your current novel idea. Who will be your major protagonists? What major events might take place? Does the synopsis seem interesting enough to sustain a novel-length work? Don't worry if your story idea morphs throughout the next few weeks. Your final synopsis may resemble nothing of this one; however, the goal for now is to come up with a cohesive, holistic vision of what your book may look like.

DAY 5: *Setting the Setting*

Famed poet and writer Marianne Moore once described poetry as "the art of creating imaginary gardens with real toads." This dictum, of course, can easily be applied to the craft of fiction writing. As writers, we must create imaginary worlds that *feel* so real to the reader that he or she becomes invested in your work and believes this world really exists somewhere beyond the page. Perhaps you've felt this way, too: After you've closed a book like *To Kill a Mockingbird*, you want to believe there actually exists a small southern town named Maycomb where the likes of people named Boo, Atticus, Scout, and Jem still live. Or maybe, in your mind, you believe you really could take a summer holiday in East or West Egg (though you've heard the rental prices are sky-high during the summer months). Perhaps you'd run into Daisy or Tom Buchanan there. I'm sure millions of people—teens and adults alike—wish they could someday visit the Shire to say hello to Bilbo Baggins and his hobbit friends or dream to someday enroll themselves or their children at Hogwarts School of Witchcraft and Wizardry. Universal Studios is betting over $250 million on the latter, in fact, for its addition to one of their theme parks that "re-creates" this fantastical setting from J.K. Rowling's books.

We've spent some time in the previous lessons discussing character and plot—the who and what of your novel—but what about the where and the when? Certainly, this is an integral decision, too. How would *To Kill a Mockingbird* have differed had it been set in New York City? What if *The Great Gatsby* took place on Planet Nebulon12XX12? These would have been different novels entirely, of course. Remember, Maycomb, East/West Egg, she Shire, and Hogwarts School of Witchcraft and Wizardry were all figments of their authors' imaginations until they were banged out, bit by bit, onto a typewriter or computer.

Your novel's setting is not simply the backdrop of your novel. The choices you make about where and when to set your novel—just as the choices you make about all other aspects of your novel—are not arbitrary ones, and so it's important to consider the kind of work that setting can and should be doing within your work.

Fiction mirrors reality in several ways, and setting is one of them. Where a character lives, for instance, and how he or she chooses to decorate, clean, organize, and arrange their living space, for example, can say a good deal about that individual. For example, as I type this, I'm looking at my office space. Stacks of student essays, yet to be graded, are piled high on my desk. Some printed articles, research for a novel-in-progress, are scattered across my floor. Aside from my keyboard, you can barely see my desk. Here are some coffee mugs, there are some pens, here is a dictionary, there are some bills. What does this description say about me and my living habits? How might you extend this to a description of my personality? Wait, don't answer that. Stop!

Instead let's take a look at an excerpt from the oft-anthologized short story "The Yellow Wallpaper" written by Charlotte Perkins Gilman in 1892. This story revolves around a woman with "a slight hysterical tendency" who is put on bed rest in the former nursery of an old mansion she and her husband have rented for the summer:

> It is a big, airy room, the whole floor nearly, with windows that look all ways, and air and sunshine galore. It was nursery first and then playroom and gymnasium, I should judge; for the windows are barred for little children, and there are rings and things in the walls.
>
> The paint and paper look as if a boys' school had used it. It is stripped off—the paper—in great patches all around the head of my bed, about as far as I can reach, and in a great place on the other side of the room low down. I never saw a worse paper in my life. One of those sprawling flamboyant patterns committing every artistic sin.
>
> It is dull enough to confuse the eye in following, pronounced enough to constantly irritate and provoke study, and when you follow the lame uncertain curves for a little distance they suddenly commit suicide—plunge off at outrageous angles, destroy themselves in unheard of contradictions.
>
> The color is repellent, almost revolting; a smouldering unclean yellow, strangely faded by the slow-turning sunlight.
>
> It is a dull yet lurid orange in some places, a sickly sulphur tint in others.
>
> No wonder the children hated it! I should hate it myself if I had to live in this room long.

The first description of the room where the protagonist is confined offers up a clear description: The walls are barred, the wallpaper is flamboyantly patterned and irritates the eye. The color of the room is revolting, unclean, sickly looking. It should come as no surprise, then, to the astute reader, that the description of this room, the setting, soon becomes representative of the narrator's state of mind. (I won't give away the ending, but the narrator kind of loses it....)

Where your own characters live and how they choose to decorate their home will say a lot about them. Does your character decorate the room with expensive nineteenth-century artwork in gilded frames? Or does he tack beer posters depicting scantily clad women in the living room? Does he live in a mansion, a house, an apartment, a cave? (Think of Ralph Ellison's *Invisible Man*; the protagonist in this novel lives in a closed-off basement room in a building that allows for only white tenants to live there.) All these choices will say something about your character's personality, habits, and values.

In addition to revealing aspects of your character's personality, setting can also expose the mood of your character. Have you ever noticed that when you're in a foul mood, you are more likely to observe the uglier side of things, such as stained carpets or crooked teeth on the woman who is smiling at you? When you are feeling upbeat, however, you notice things such as the dew-touched flowers, the sun peeking out of the clouds, the gentle rustle of leaves in the warm fall breeze. Take, for instance, this one-line description of setting in the final pages of *Love in the Time of Cholera* when Florentino Ariza is finally reunited with the woman he loves after fifty-three years, seven months, and eleven days (yes, he's counted): "Then he looked through the windows at the complete circle of the quadrant on the mariner's compass, the clear horizon, the December sky without a single cloud, the waters that could be navigated forever...."

Though subtle, Florentino's state of mind is reflected in this description. The sky is blue, cloudless, clear. Florentino's in love, and he's noticing the beauty in the world. How might his perspective have changed had he just been defeated in love? Perhaps he wouldn't even be able to see past the window; perhaps he'd focus only the dirt and finger smudges that were standing between him and an empty sky. Setting is every bit a matter of perspective, and perspective reflects of the temperament of the viewer.

Additionally, setting can mark the tone of a scene. How would a story that begins on a dark and stormy night differ from one that begins in the first days of spring, when tulips begin poking out of the ground like eager tongues? They'd differ greatly, of course.

But don't forget that setting isn't simply about where the story is taking place, but also *when*. The time period of your story will dictate the social conventions of the day— attitudes, styles, and lingo. If you choose to set your novel in the past, you're going to have to do a bit of research. In what time period would a character likely say "Far out!" or "Groovy!" or "Rad!" or "Cool!" or "Sweet!" when responding in an excited way? What were the prevailing cultural, political, or social thoughts? How might *The Invisible Man* differ now if it were rewritten in modern times?

Consistency is important in creating your imaginary world, even if your fictional setting has no basis in reality. Be certain you aren't simply placing your characters on an empty backdrop devoid of any real meaning. Use setting to orient your reader, reveal character traits, expose moods, and set the tone.

Assignment

The goal of this assignment is to examine the various uses of setting in your work.

First, select at least three of your characters from your bios and write a description of where they live. Keep in mind that where your character lives and how she decorates and/or maintains her home will go a ways toward uncovering her personality. Try to provide as many sensory details as possible. What does your character see, hear, smell, or feel? After you've done this, write a description of each character's favorite space. Is it an art gallery? A park? A church? What do you think attracts your character to this space?

Next, using one of the plot points in the synopsis you've written for yesterday's lesson, write a scene that specifically uses setting to reveal the mood of the character and the tone of the scene. How can you utilize setting to reflect your character's interiority in subtle ways?

Finally, do a bit of research on the time period of your novel—even if you've set your novel in contemporary culture. What kind of details can you add to make your story realistic? Are your characters wearing skinny jeans or bell-bottoms? Tie-dye or girdles? Now write a short scene, separate from the one you've already written, incorporating some of your research.

DAY 6: *The Heart of the Heart of Your Novel*

Let's face it—the word *sentimental*, nowadays, is used to describe a negative impression a reader might have about a novel. "Sentimental" is often launched as an insult, meaning the story was a bit too precious, or tugged on the heartstrings in a transparent, saccharine, sweet way. However, it's important to note the difference between sentimental and sentiment. The former turns off readers, the latter draws them in.

An emotional core is absolutely necessary to any good novel—otherwise, why should your readers even care? Think about the novels that have stayed with you long after you've read them. Perhaps a reason you felt such a connection to the work is because you connected, emotionally, with the main character. You, too, have experienced heartbreak, or disappointment, or loneliness, or confusion, or affection like theirs.

Many novels hinge upon internal tension or conflict—derived, of course, from emotional complexity. Think of our example of Daisy Buchanan; she loves two people at once: Gatsby and her husband. These conflicting desires cause much turmoil in the novel—yet they are mostly internally driven. But how do writers convey the range of emotions that a novel should contain? Well, with practice, of course. First, writers must learn the difference between writing emotions and simply writing *about* emotions.

Let's remind ourselves again of Mark Twain's sage advice, "Don't tell us that the old lady screamed. Bring her on and let her scream." Twain knew very well that readers don't want to be told how to think or how to feel—instead they want to experience emotions and sensations vicariously through the characters themselves. A reader who is told that "Billy felt sad" will likely not feel the weight of his sadness. However your reader most certainly will feel Billy's sorrow if he experiences it with him, through physical descriptions. Writing emotions asks you to trust your reader enough to intuit your character's emotional state through his physical state.

Think of a time you felt an intense emotion. Let's say you were angry. ANGRY-ANGRY. What did you do? How did you feel? Did you clench your teeth so tightly that your jaw began to hurt? Was your face red and hot to the touch? Were the muscles in your neck and face tensed up, so you felt a bit like a sand-stuffed hacky sack? Were your hands balled into fists that felt like rocks? I'm sure you've experienced at least some of these sensations. The takeaway is this: All emotions, even your own, are experienced through physical sensations.

Instead of writing, "Billy felt sad," describe exactly how he feels this sadness on a physical level. Does his mouth feel like it's stuffed with cotton balls? Do his eyes sting? Does his heart feel like it has sunken into his stomach and is now being digested by his stomach acids? Does the world suddenly feel empty and quiet—does the air feel weighty around his body? It will be precisely through these physical sensations that you'll be able to connect your reader to the internal workings of your characters.

One key to writing about emotion is focusing on word choice. Mark Twain, again, has some wise words to share with us. Twain once noted, "The difference between the right word and the almost right word is … the difference between the lightning bug and the lightning." Twain's advice here should be taken to heart, especially with matters of the heart. Be sure you're paying particular attention to word choice as you describe the emotions of your character in any given scene. Does Billy storm out of the room? Stagger out of the room? Lumber out of the room? Totter out of the room? Crawl out of the room? Each of these words has a unique connotation, and selecting the right word—not the almost-right word, as Twain advises us—is going to make all the difference.

Take a look at how Ian McEwan, in his novel-turned-major-motion-picture, *Atonement*, captures the essence of his character's emotions. If you've read this novel—or even seen the movie—you'll remember the early scene in the library, where Briony, the novel's child-protagonist, witnesses her sister, Celia, making love to her suitor, Robbie. Several scenes later, Briony finds her cousin Lola, who has just been raped in the woods near her house by an unknown attacker. McEwan writes:

> Lola was sitting forward, with her arms crossed around her chest, hugging herself and rocking slightly. The voice was faint and distorted, as though impeded by something like a bubble, some mucus in her throat. She needed to clear her throat. She said, vaguely, "I'm sorry, I didn't, I'm sorry..."

Lola's body language, her muddled voice, and the feeling of mucus in her throat resonate with the reader in a way that stating, "She was shocked" simply would not. We can almost hear that weak voice, muffled by a mucousy lump in her throat—and this is enough to tell us what we need to know about Lola's current state of mind.

But emotion can be conveyed in other ways. You've heard the saying "Actions speak louder than words." How your character acts and reacts to the events before him, and what he says directly, will tell the reader something about your character. This may seem an obvious point, but it's one worth considering. Let's continue reading this same scene from *Atonement*. This time I've labeled in brackets where emotion is being conveyed:

> Briony whispered, "Who was it?" and before that could be answered, she added, with all the calm she was capable of, "I saw him. I *saw* him." [Dialogue; hints at Briony's pressuring]
> Meekly, Lola said," Yes." [Dialogue that characterizes; Lola is impressionable]

For the second time that evening, Briony felt a flowering of tenderness for her cousin. Together they faced real terrors. She and her cousin were close. Briony was on her knees, trying to put her arms round Lola and gather her to her, but the body was bony and unyielding, wrapped tight about itself like a seashell. A wrinkle. Lola hugged herself and rocked. [Emotion through description]

Briony said, "It was him, wasn't it?" [Briony wants Lola to label her attacker as Robbie, but Lola is reticent]

She felt against her chest, rather than saw, her cousin nod, slowly, reflectively. [Emotion through physical description] Perhaps it was exhaustion.

After many seconds Lola said in the same weak, submissive voice, "Yes. It was him." [Resolution to scene; Lola concedes to falsely asserting that Robbie was her attacker]

In this scene, we learn a lot about Briony through both her brief clips of dialogue and her actions.

Briony, having earlier witnessed her sister having sex with Robbie, has conflated these two events, and she pressures Lola to name Robbie as her attacker. At this point, we learn that the novel is headed along a tragic arc, not a romantic or fanciful one—and it just might be Briony we have to blame for the results. Her foolish, girlish ego, her desire to be inquisitive, to be in the know, is about to wreak havoc with the lives of people she loves. Emotions like juvenile jealousy—Briony has a crush on Robbie and knows he loves her sister—will push aside reason, cause unexpected action, create conflict, and mask the truth. To atone, after all, one must have done something terribly, horribly wrong, and then, of course, feel remorseful for those actions.

How might this novel have taken a different direction had Briony's words or actions taken a different trajectory in this particular scene? What if Briony only acted in a way that showed concern for Lola, instead of immediately seeking the name of her assailant? Had Briony run to find an adult or simply helped Lola to her feet and back to the house, her actions would have portrayed her as sympathetic, noble, and compassionate.

But then there wouldn't have been much of a novel, would there? One reason, I imagine, that so many viewers and readers connected with *Atonement* is that they related to the range of emotions they faced: Love, lies, strife, loneliness, guilt, pain—these are the complexities of the human condition and the central complication of the novel.

Assignment

The goal of this assignment is to practice conveying emotion through physical description, dialogue, and action. Remember—never tell your reader exactly what a character is feeling. Instead let emotions evolve organically through description and action.

First, to warm up, select at least three of your characters from your bios and write a short scene for each wherein the character is experiencing a deep emotion—fear, anger, sadness, devastation, guilt. Try your best to convey this emotion only through physical sensation and action.

Next, write a short scene where one of the characters above is feeling a strong emotion, but is in a public place and can't reveal it adequately. (Perhaps she is having a panic attack at a job interview but wants to convey confidence. Or perhaps she is in an important business meeting but just learned her newlywed husband is having an affair.)

Finally, write a longer scene involving two or more characters. In this scene, at least one of your characters must want something he/she cannot have. (You may want to revisit some of your bios to remind yourself of your character's yearnings and motivations.) As your characters deal with strong emotions, what you come up with may surprise you. You may be developing important plot points for your novel.

DAY 7: *Say What?! Some Tips on Dialogue*

In an earlier lesson, we cited character formation as the single most important aspect in all novels. We then spent the next few days thinking about how your characters will be revealed through their actions and motivations, how to use setting to explore the mood and personality of your characters, and how to best convey the inner sentiments of those characters. By now you know that an emotional core, derived from your characters' internal lives, is fundamental to any complex and interesting story.

One problem I've noticed in my students' writings is that they create really interesting, complex, nuanced characters, but they fail to engage them with any of their other characters. In their "real lives" most people tend to be non-confrontational—especially writer types—and sometimes this rubs off in their writing as well. If you create interesting characters, don't confine them to their own heads; let them walk, talk, and interact with the other characters you've created.

What a person says, too, can go a long way toward revealing her character. Perhaps your character wants to seem smart, so she tries using unusually big words, only to misuse them: "That bombastic cupcake is ostentatiously scrumptious, I decry!" If a character is a scientist or a doctor, perhaps he uses technical terms. Instead of saying "My wife is pregnant," he might explain, "My spousal partner has a fetus in utero." Or if a character is an auto mechanic, perhaps he uses metaphors suited for his profession: "That'd be as embarrassing as an El Dorado with a rusted muffler." Oh, boy. That *is* embarrassing

Consider, too, when what a character *says* differs from what he *thinks*:

> "I love you," said Penelope.
> "Uh ... I love you, too," Ricky said, because he didn't know what else to say. He watched her snap her gum, and in this moment she looked even more like a horse. He needed to find a way to let her down easy.

When done artfully, a scene of dialogue can make a reader feel like she is in the room with Penelope and Ricky, cringing at the awkwardness of the exchange. When done poorly, rest assured the reader will be cringing at the author's ill attempt at writing dialogue. Remember, dialogue should sound true to life, and everyone speaks differently. Be sure your dialogue is distinctive and authentic to the character doing the speaking.

Your written dialogue should always be working to reveal the depth, intentions, or actions of your character. A common mistake is using dialogue as "filler" that simply describes the setting or narrates the plot. Consider this scene:

> "What is the weather like outside today?" asked Penelope.
> "The sky is blue, and the silhouettes of ducks taking flight to the south are lovely, like planes flying overhead," said Ricky.
> "I am going to get in my car and drive to the hair salon," said Penelope. "My strawberry-blonde hair could use a good cut."

"Wait, I hear a knock on the door," said Ricky. "Why, it's the mailman, and he has an important letter from my dying aunt. What's this? She's dead. But she's left me her estate! I'm rich! See you later, horse-face! Don't let the door hit you on the way out!"

A scene such as this one will quickly lead your reader to skip these pages or put down your book altogether. A good general rule to follow when allowing your characters to speak directly is this: Dialogue should always aim to reveal some character trait about the individual who is speaking. If your character speaks a line of dialogue in order to describe the setting, this description should also reveal an element of your character's interiority. What does Ricky's line of dialogue about the lovely ducks flying south reveal about him? Does it indicate that he's sensitive? If so, why does he call his girlfriend "horse-face"? If the spoken line of description doesn't tell us much about your character, that line will be better served in a paragraph of exposition. Dialogue should accomplish two things at once: Describe a setting *and* tell us something about a character; convey plot-forwarding action *and* provide the reader with your character's history; establish tone *and* show how your character's dialogue conflicts with his indirect thoughts. However, each line of dialogue should give your reader insight into your character's mind, personality, or motivations.

Here are some other general rules to follow when writing a dialogue scene:

- Avoid beginning a scene with a line of dialogue. It's a good idea to first orient your reader to the setting and who is present at the scene. Readers process information in the order they receive it, so if you launch into dialogue before setting the scene, they may not know who is speaking and to whom.

- Be sure to describe what your character is doing while he is speaking. When Ricky tells Penelope that he loves her, is he looking at the floor? Is he flipping through channels on the television set?

- Be sure to give some insight into what the characters are thinking versus what they are saying. Such a contrast will provide tension in your scene.

- Be sure to balance dialogue with descriptions of setting and paragraphs of exposition. Dialogue scenes are often a great place to "sneak in" sentences of exposition and character history that might stand out if contained in a separate paragraph. For example:

> "I love you, too," Ricky said. He doubted there was such a thing as love. His ex-wife told him she loved him all the time, all the while sleeping with his brother, Mickey.

- Less is more when it comes to dialogue. People don't often speak in long paragraphs. At least not without some breaks. Dialogue scenes can quicken the pace of a novel and give your reader a needed rest from long paragraphs of exposition or description.

- Your characters should all speak differently from one another. If you randomly extracted a line of dialogue from your novel, you should be able to tell to whom it belongs simply by analyzing the diction, content, and tone.

- Make sure you include dialogue tags so we know who is speaking and to whom. A simple "he said" or "she said" usually works best and does not draw attention to itself as "He pontificated wildly" might. Your goal is to aim for invisibility when writing dialogue tags, so this is not the best place to demonstrate your creativity.

- Avoid too many adverbs in your dialogue tags that tell your reader how to "interpret" a line of dialogue. Consider this example: "'I hate you, I hate you, I hate you, Ricky!' Penelope said angrily after Ricky insulted her equine mug." If Penelope is saying something as strong as "I hate you, I hate you, I hate you," we can assume she's saying it angrily. Your dialogue should be able to, pardon the pun, speak for itself. Trust that your reader will "get" it.

- Avoid overusing exclamation points! These can be easily distracting and irritating to your reader! Plus, it makes it seem like your characters are breathlessly exclaiming something, when this isn't always the case! Punctuation should, like dialogue tags, never draw attention to itself! Never ever!

- Always read your dialogue out loud. When you do this, you'll be able to pick up on awkward phrases and dialogue that sounds stilted. It will also help you generate ideas.

Assignment

The goal of this assignment is to practice engaging your characters with other characters, and, in addition, to practice writing dialogue to reveal elements of your characters. Keep in mind that what a person says, how she says it, or how it conflicts with her internal musings will do a lot of the muscle work of character development.

First, think of some real individuals you've come into contact with today (waitress, coat-check girl, car-wash attendant, etc.) and place them each in a scene with one of your characters. How will these individuals interact? What might they discuss? You never know when one of these "minor contacts" will have a big impact on a more prominent character. (And if you find one of these minor characters interesting, you may wish to draw up a separate character bio.)

Next, write a short dialogue scene involving your two characters *least likely* to interact in your novel. What might they discuss? You never know when you might learn something about these characters that you didn't know before. (And if you do learn something important, be sure to update your character bio to reflect this.)

Finally, write a dialogue scene involving at least two of your characters who are directly at odds with one another. For now, don't worry if you don't actually envision this as a scene in your novel. Just focus on integrating action, descriptions of setting, and descriptions of your characters' body language. After you've finished, review the general rules for integrating dialogue. Did you adhere to these?

DAY 8: *Choosing Your Eyeballs*

By now, you've been hard at work on your novel for over a week! If you're not accustomed to such a rigorous writing schedule, you may feel exhausted and eager for some praise. So I say: Good job. Go ahead and pat yourself on the back. But then get back to work. Hopefully, if you've been dedicating yourself to at least two hours of writing each day, your excellent progress is reward enough. Keep writing. You are only a fraction of the way there. (⁷⁄₉₀ths to be exact.)

In previous assignments, you were asked to consider some of the primary actors in your novel. And maybe by now you know who will stand out as the central characters in your story. But who is actually going to tell your story? Which point of view (POV) will you use? Whose head will you allow your reader to access? The point of view is going to be an essential decision you'll want to make fairly early on in the novel-writing process. Essentially, POV is the perspective from which your story is narrated.

Keep in mind that the character you choose to narrate your novel will affect the overall voice, tone, and style of your work. It will also affect *how* the story gets told, what events are emphasized or deemphasized, and how the events are filtered, through the character, to your reader. For instance, how might *To Kill a Mockingbird* have changed if it weren't narrated by Scout, a child at the time of the novel's main events? Scout is both innocent and nonjudgmental, which clearly comes to bear on the narrating of the events itself. How might *The Great Gatsby* have been less effective had Jay Gatsby himself been the narrator? What about the recent novel *The Lovely Bones*? This novel is narrated by Susie Salmon, who announces from the novel's first sentence that she's already dead and narrating from the great beyond. The novel would have been an entirely different entity altogether had a different narrator taken the helm—and quite possibly, the novel wouldn't have been as enormously popular. One reason readers are drawn in so quickly, I imagine, is because of the unique point of view.

So I'll say it again: Whom you choose to tell your story will have a dramatic impact on the story itself.

Consider this scenario:

Three people are in a diner: a waitress, a male customer at the counter, whose face is badly disfigured, and a female customer at a window table in the corner. Coffee is spilled on the male customer at the counter. "I'm going to send you the bill for my dry cleaning! No—I'll SUE you," the man yells before he leaves. "Never come back here again!" yells the waitress at the same time.

Now let's consider this scenario from each varying point of view.

- The man at the counter feels self-conscious because of his face—scarred in a house fire set by his ex-wife. Since then, he's harbored a misogynistic attitude toward women. He was watching the waitress, but then he saw that look in her eyes: pity and disgust. She couldn't disguise it, he imagined. "More coffee?" she asked him, holding out the pot. He leans in slightly to whisper something, but he never gets the chance to say it. The waitress seems startled by him—it's his face, he assumes—and that's when she intentionally spilled his cup of coffee down his suit.

- The waitress behind the counter was recently mugged after her morning shift at the diner. The man said he had a gun, though she never saw it, and he promised he'd be back if she called the police. Nevertheless, she phoned 911 that night as soon as she could find a phone. She's a bit on edge, and she's recently been seeing a therapist for it. The man at the counter is making her nervous, though he seems nice enough. He said please and thank you when he ordered his coffee. If she can just get through the day, then she can go home to the safety of her apartment. "More coffee?" she asked him, holding out the pot, but when he leaned in to whisper something, she thought it could be HIM, the man who mugged her. Her arms grew weak. She dropped the coffee cup.

- The woman at the window is watching the people pass by on the street outside. She's tired and waiting for her order of huevos rancheros. She notices the disfigured man at the counter and doesn't want to seem to stare. Suddenly, she looks up and hears them both yelling. All over a cup of spilled coffee. Some people just take things too seriously, she thinks.

As you can see, each of the above scenarios offers a particular angle of vision. The POV can be defined as the bias of the person telling the story. The history and background of the individual that is influencing the relaying of the story. The particular lens through which the story is told. What can that individual actually see? What is influencing him or her? What can't be seen, and what's left out?

The waitress believes the disfigured man at the counter was the man who robbed her. The disfigured man, in his state of hyperself-consciousness, believes the woman is looking at him in disgust and pity. The woman at the window, however, has missed much of the action. From her vantage point, she can see only certain things, and she might have missed the subtle exchange between the man and the waitress. Her response: *What's the big deal?*

When selecting your POV character, you should ask yourself these questions:

- Whose POV is the most interesting? In the scenario above, I can tell you whose perspective is *least* interesting: the woman at the window, who barely notices the events unfolding.

- What is the POV character's motivation for telling the story?

- What is your POV character's relationship to the protagonist? Is he the protagonist?

- From what narrative distance is the POV character telling the story? That is, how much time has elapsed since the telling of the events? Think of the popular television show *The Wonder Years*. If you recall, that show was narrated by a man, grown well into his adult years, looking back with nostalgia at his childhood. This nostalgia certainly tempered his retelling of events. *Atonement*, too, is told from the narrative distance of decades as the protagonist, Briony, looks back with regret on the events that transpired in her early years. You should ask yourself what the perspective of time has done for the telling of the story.

- Who can be present at the most important (and climatic) moments in the novel, so as to narrate these events to the reader? This is a logistical decision, of course. If a character dies midway through your novel, he clearly cannot narrate the rest of the events—unless, of course, he does so from the grave. Spooky.

Keep in mind that your POV character does not need to be the protagonist of your novel (consider, again, Jay Gatsby/ Nick Carraway). In the case of Jay Gatsby—he might have been too convinced by his own lies and misrepresentations to be a very reliable narrator.

Assignment

The goal of this exercise is to demonstrate that the choices you make about point of view will affect *how* your story is told. First, select three characters from your character bios and put them in a short (no longer than three pages) scene together. In this scene, at least one of your characters should discover something that will change his or her life (either for the positive or the negative). Perhaps a character has discovered that he won $42,000 and a lifetime of free stays at the Hilton, Paris, on a nationally televised game show. While he's overjoyed, another character might be envious or spiteful. Remember, you'll be writing this scene multiple times, so consider the inner thoughts and motivations of each character.

In the first draft, write this scene from the perspective of character one. In the second draft, write this scene from the perspective of character two. In the third draft, write this scene from the perspective of character three. When you have completed each scene, I want you to write a paragraph of assessment. Which perspective did you find the most natural? Which perspective offers the most interesting vantage point? If you were starting your novel today, which of these three characters would you select to narrate it?

DAY 9: *POV&V (Point of View and Voice)*

Yesterday we learned a bit about how to select the best point of view (POV) character for your novel, and, hopefully, after several days of writing exercises, you're getting closer to recognizing who that character should be. However, several other aspects of POV should also be taken into consideration when outlining and drafting your novel. (I know, I know: So much to think about, so little time!) After selecting your POV character, you must then decide which POV *type* is best for your work. Then, depending on which character you choose to narrate your work, and how, your narrative voice can be adjusted accordingly.

But first things first. Following is a brief primer on the main types of narration:

FIRST PERSON: Narrated from the perspective of "I."

Example: *I dropped the coffee on the customer because I was nervous; I thought he was the man who mugged me.*

Consider the first line from *Moby-Dick*: "Call me Ishmael." Immediately, we know that this first-person narrator, kindly enough to allow us to call him by his first name, is going to walk us through the events of the story. While the first-person POV lends us an immediacy (readers often experience the events of the novel with the narrator as he participates in the story), usually, this perspective is limited to one person's thoughts and observations.

A strength of the first-person narration can be found in the immediacy of the storytelling itself. The first-person narrator speaks directly to the reader without the third party of the author rearing her pesky head into the story. However, this perspective is also extremely limited. So, that is to say, because we are in the "head" of Ishmael in *Moby-Dick*, we cannot know the thoughts of other characters such as Captain Ahab, Starbuck, or Queequeg—unless they tell Ishmael directly, and he, in turn, tells us. (And unless they're being perfectly honest with him about what they're thinking.) Also, first person can, at times, be unreliable as narrators often hold a deep bias in relation to the story being told.

THIRD PERSON, LIMITED: Narrated from the perspective of "he" or "she." This type of narration follows a single character from a slight distance and is privy to that single character's thoughts and observations but not the thoughts and observations of others.

Example: *She dropped the coffee on the disfigured man because she was nervous, thinking he was the man who mugged her.*

Third person is probably the most popular narrative mode, and for good reason. This type of narration provides added flexibility when conveying a story to your reader. No longer are you limited to the eyewitness account of a single first-person narrator (ex: *I saw her drop the coffee*), but the narrator can objectively report the actions of the story (vis-à-vis the external actions of all characters) while at the same time having access to one character's internal musings.

This type of POV also most closely approximates the way a reader interprets the real world. Unless we have telepathic or clairvoyant powers, we are not privy to the interior thoughts of those who surround us. (And thank goodness, I say! That'd be a mess.) Third person allows us to lose ourselves in the story, observing as we would in real life (he said *what?!?!*) the actions that unfold before us.

THIRD PERSON, OMNISCIENT: Also narrated from the perspective of "he" or "she." However, with this type of narration, we can pop in and out of the heads of multiple characters. This is also known as godlike narration.

Example: *She dropped the coffee on the man because she was nervous. She saw him leaning in to say something, and she had a feeling he was the mugger. What she didn't know what that he felt betrayed when she looked at him with those eyes of pity. His heart had sunk into his chest, and he was struck with the idea that he'd never be loved.*

In an omniscient narration, the reader knows the thoughts and observations of more than one character. And, additionally, this type of narration isn't as constrained, for an omniscient narrator can jump back and forth in time and space, visit the "head" of one character, then show us what another is thinking. While this may be useful in creating a rich narrative—this is, after all, the prime POV mode for the Bible, epics such as *The Lord of the Rings* trilogy, and many nineteenth-century texts—switching POVs too frequently can cause confusion. And, more to the point, many modern-day readers don't like to be told *everything*. There is such a thing as letting your reader know *too much* about what everyone thinks at every plot point that might ruin the magic of the story itself.

The narrative voice of your novel is going to greatly depend on the POV character and type of narration you decide upon, and these decisions should be made prior to writing a single word of your outline or a single sentence of your novel. The narrative voice can be loosely defined as the way your POV character's personality is coming across the page. Think again about the lessons of dialogue we learned on Day 7. Each character has a distinctive way of speaking that is the sum of his personality, background, education, and experiences. These qualities, too, will come through when narrating the events of the story itself in the form of diction, cadence, sentence length, and style. Is your narrator confident and proud? Overly self-conscious and self-deprecating? Guilty and confessional? Dominating as a peacock?

Consider the first few lines from the iconic classic *The Catcher in the Rye* written by the late, great J.D. Salinger:

> If you really want to hear about it, the first thing you'll probably want to know is where I was born, and what my lousy childhood was like, and how my parents were occupied and all before they had me, and all that David Copperfield kind of crap, but I don't feel like going into it, if you want to know the truth. In the first place, that stuff bores me, and in the second place, my parents would have about two hemorrhages apiece if I told anything pretty personal about them.

In these first sentences alone the voice of the novel's protagonist, Holden Caulfield, presents itself loud and clear. What kind of individual would use diction such as "David Copperfield kind of crap" and "my parents would have two hemorrhages"? Who would write in long, rambling, breathless sentences? This isn't a young boy who is naive in the way youth often are; he's jaded and cynical. In fact, he gives definition to the term *teen angst*.

Even though it may seem premature to consider the narrative voice of your yet-to-be-outlined novel, this consideration is so closely linked to how the story will be told, to the perspective, and to character, it's impossible to develop your novel without some serious consideration.

Assignment

The goal of today's assignment is to explore potential POV types and the effect they may have on your novel. In yesterday's assignment, you were asked to write one scene from the perspective of three different characters. Today I want you to choose one of those scenes (perhaps the one you felt was the most interesting or compelling) and rewrite it from the first-person, third-person limited, and third-person-omniscient point of views. Then reread all your scenes and ask yourself which one feels the most natural.

Then select the character you will most likely use as your POV character. (Remember, until you begin to write your outline, your POV may change. For now, simply focus on the exploration and development of each exercise.) Write what might be the first scene of your novel using this character, selecting a POV type and focusing on developing the voice of the character. When you reread this exercise, you should decipher—through the style, diction, rhythm, and sentence structure—some personality traits of your character. Try integrating some of your learnings from previous exercises into this scene: How can you convey your character's emotions? How can you engage this character in direct conversation with another character? Write freely, and don't overthink it—you never know where your character might take you or what you might discover through the process.

DAY 10: *Packing Enough Baggage*

Perhaps you just want to get on with it—you want to write your novel, already, and here we are on Day 10 without even a working outline. Hold your horses, Nelly. Make like a yogi and practice the art of watchful waiting. Channel Mr. Miyagi. You still have plenty to consider, and remember: The work you do now will make the actual writing of the novel progress much faster and smoother.

You no doubt learned a great deal about your main players in the past several days, but before you get too deeply into writing your novel, you should make sure your characters are complex, interesting, and likable enough to sustain a novel. Perhaps no greater blow could be dealt to a novel than when a reader reports, "I just didn't care about the characters." I cannot emphasize enough how important your characters are to your novel, even if you are writing a plot-driven novel, such as an action novel or a crime drama. Without interesting characters, your reader will be left asking, "Who the heck cares?" (And they'll answer: "Not me.")

Character History

So, before you get too far into the process, don't forget to pack! Your character's baggage, that is. Let's face it: We all have our baggage. Maybe Deak is still not over his wife's affair in the months after their wedding. Or maybe the plane crash Candy was in as a child psychologically scarred her for life. Did Geeta's absentee father give her "daddy issues" that sent her to seek comfort in the arms of men she meets out at bars? Uh-huh. You got that right.

Just as human beings are the sum of our histories and experiences, so, too, are our characters. You'll need to know your character's background, his childhood traumas, his likes and dislikes, and his fears. You've done some of this work already with your character bios—and this is all good work. But it takes more than a night's worth of bio writing to create complex characters. You'll have to know the experiences that have defined him—prior to the present time of your novel. For example, would Jody, a young professional whose twin brother died in a sledding accident when he was young, be more or less likely to become a professional skier? Would he be more or less likely to let his own children go sledding during the first snow?

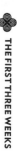

Would he be more or less likely to live somewhere snowy? Depending on his experiences and how they impacted him, the answers will vary.

Complex characters will carry a novel much further than simple, one-dimensional ones. With the exception of Forrest Gump, I can think of no single fictional protagonist who is not deeply complicated. (And Gump is complex in his own way—he's a simple man, but with great ambitions. And he knows what love is.)

Take out the character bios you wrote for Day 2 and examine them for a moment. Which of the characters you've studied is the most complex? Which is the most likable or interesting? And, on the other side—who might not be compelling enough to write about? How has each been shaped by his or her experiences? In your assignments since Day 2, which characters do you find yourself writing the most about? Which ones keep returning to your mind while you're not writing?

Character Appearance

Maybe your mother or father told you this when you were younger: "It's what's on the inside that counts." Or maybe they said this: "Beauty is only skin deep." What parents sometimes neglect to tell their children is that appearance—what's on the outside—often reflects our personality, attitudes, and values. Looks *do* matter, at least from the standpoint of ascertaining, via judgment calls (which aren't always right), what that individual might be like. For example, a man with long, stringy hair and a goatee will make an impression quite different from a man in a pressed suit and slicked-back hair. One might be found at a Phish show, the other in an executive suite. One might smoke marijuana and strum his guitar, while the other drinks a nightcap of Scotch while he watches ESPN. One might ride a bicycle to work, while the other drives a brand-new BMW. One might shop at Salvation Army, the other at Crate & Barrel.

What a character looks like, and even his body language, goes a long way toward showing the reader what a character is like. Does your character walk with a limp? Does he hunch his shoulders? Does your character move her lips stiffly, too embarrassed to show her teeth? You'll need to start thinking about the physical features of your characters and what they tell the reader about your character's interiority. If your character has dark, foreboding eyes, for instance, is this a sign of a more malevolent interior? Is this character innately bad? If your character has porcelain skin, does this mean she's pure of heart? Or that she never played outdoor sports as a result of a hovering, overprotective mother who never left the house without three bottles of SPF 80?

Simply put, the point is this: Writers need to be aware of the choices we're making as just that: choices. Sometimes in the fugue of writing we forget to stop and ponder just *why* we're making the choices we are making. The way your character walks, speaks, dresses, and acts will all help make her leap off the page. (Unless your character is old and sickly, in which case she might hobble off the page. Or fall. But you get the point.)

Character Motive

All characters—and most certainly your central characters—must have motivation. They must want something. Romeo wants Juliet. The Count of Monte Cristo wants revenge. (Or an excellent, fattening sandwich.) But what does your protagonist want? Left with no desires and no motivation, your novel will become a desolate wasteland, and you'll waste a good chunk of these next eighty days spinning your wheels.

Motivation forces your novel, and your characters, by extension, forward. It propels the plot. What does your character want most in this world, and how does this wanting affect how he reacts in particular situations? We've discussed this already, but it's an important point to hammer home. Yearning generates plot.

However, it is in our human nature, most of the time, unless you are a narcissist or sociopath, to want what is best for our fellow humans. Certainly, we want what is best for our friends and loved ones. After spending so much time with your characters, well, they *feel* like loved ones. Thus, shouldn't you want the best for them, too?

Not if you want a compelling story.

Take out a sticky note and write on it: Do not give (fill in the blank with your protagonist's name) what he/she wants! Post this to your keyboard or to the bottom of your computer screen.

Character Likability/Plausibility

Two last points of consideration ask you to put yourself into the shoes of your reading audience. (You should always do this unconsciously, of course.) First, an audience must like your protagonist, even if he or she does some "bad" things. Overly perfect people come off the page as downright annoying, as are individuals who are preachy or know-it-alls. If your central character is, essentially, "good," be sure to give him some flaws that make him seem more fully human.

I'm not suggesting your protagonists all be good guys—not at all. Scores of novels feature protagonists we would not want to invite to Thanksgiving dinner. Have you ever read a novel or seen a film when you were actually rooting for the protagonist—a "bad" guy, perhaps a criminal—to get away with some vile act? These bad guys had some redeeming qualities that attracted the reader in the first place. Think about Vladimir Nabokov's novel *Lolita*, for example. In this novel, the protagonist, Humbert Humbert, a middle-aged pedophile, seduces and carries on a multi-state whirlwind romance with the nubile—and very under-age—Lolita. Yet, as the reader turns the pages, she becomes entranced with that idiosyncratic Humbert Humbert who, in his own way, is a bit of a romantic. And the reader *can* relate to that. If Humbert Humbert had no positive qualities, no charismatic traits—nothing to signal that he, too, is human—rest assured this book would have been pulled off the shelves as quickly as you can say Lo-Lee-Ta.

Finally, all characters must maintain a level of plausibility; that is, the way that character develops throughout the novel must be authentic to the way that individual would naturally develop. For example, if in chapter one your character is an egomaniacal man with a drug habit and a gambling addiction, it is unlikely he'll decide to become a Catholic priest down the road in chapter ten, unless of course, he was doing it to get closer to some bingo halls.

Assignment

The goal of today's writing is to further develop some of our main players, making sure they have the staying power and charisma required of a novel's protagonist.

First, select a character who is likely to be your protagonist and allow yourself to freely write about him or her for a sustained period of *at least* thirty minutes to an hour. What does he look like? What is his history? What motivates him? In what ways is he a good guy with flaws or a bad guy with positive attributes? Allow yourself to more fully explore the complexity of this one character.

Next, write a scene introducing the above character as the central actor, paying particular attention to character history, complexity, motivation, and physical description. In this scene your character must want something but, of course, cannot have it. (Glance, if you must, at the sticky note you've stuck to your writing desk: Do not give the protagonist what he/she wants!)

DAY 11: *The Art of Conflict*

At this point, you should begin loosely considering how to shape the narrative arc of your novel—how your novel progresses from the beginning, to the middle, to the end. We'll be discussing narrative arc in more detail later in this book, but for now, you should begin to think about how to divide your novel into parts. All good stories—movies and novels alike—evolve as the conflict within the story gets introduced, complicated, and resolved.

We can learn a lot about writing from the movies. A movie-marathon day might yield a total sum of four movies viewed, but reading four novels would take a week or more, at least. (Unless you've mastered the art of speed reading.)

According to famous screenplay writer and teacher Syd Field, there should be two major plot points in any given movie. Plot Point 1 should occur approximately one-third of the way through the film, and Plot Point 2, the climax, should happen approximately two-thirds of the way through the film. Plot Point 1 should deepen the complication for the characters introduced in the first section—compel them to action—while Plot Point 2 is the turning point—or rather the point of no return—for the characters.

So, in the movie *Thelma and Louise*, as Field highlights, Plot Point 1, approximately thirty minutes into the movie, occurs when Louise shoots and kills the man who is attempting to rape Thelma in the parking lot of the Silver Bullet nightclub. Now these characters are *compelled* to action. Now Thelma and Louise are no longer on a road trip; they're on the run! And the viewer is running right along with them, breathlessly trying to keep up.

Although novels don't behave exactly as movies do, Syd Field's advice can be really useful to novelists and screenwriters alike. Conflict drives your novel, pushing it along at a pace that forces your reader to keep reading in order to catch up. Ask yourself: What is the first major complication your protagonist will face? What is the first conflict that compels the protagonist to action? What other conflicts will your protagonist have to go head-to-head with that will further complicate the plot? Are these external conflicts or more internal ones?

Human beings are complex creatures. Often, conflict arises from two competing desires at war within an individual. For instance, in *Thelma and Louise*, Louise was faced with a conflict at the moment she comes face-to-face with Thelma's would-be rapist in the parking lot of the Silver Bullet: Be free from responsibility and constraints *or* punish the man who is attempting to rape her best friend (the result of which will absolutely embroil her within the

constraints of the law, those chains that bind). We all know which path Louise chooses—and the ultimate outcome. (If you've not seen the movie, I won't spoil it for you. But think car. Think cliff. Think pedal to the metal.)

Nonflict is the term I use to describe those incidents in your novel that are disguised as conflict. A nonflict, quite simply, is a tension that does not necessarily result in any action or reaction from your characters. A nonflict is yearning without action. A conflict drives the story forward; a nonflict does not. Nonflict keeps you spinning your wheels (a bit like the wheels on Louise's convertible, right before it plunges off the cliff! Spoiler alert!).

Take a look at this example:

> **NONFLICT:** I love my boyfriend so much. I mean, really, I love him so much it hurts.

> **CONFLICT:** I love my boyfriend so much, but our parents forbid us from seeing each other due to an old family feud. (*Romeo and Juliet*)

> **CONFLICT:** I love my boyfriend so much, but he is married to my sister. (*Hannah and Her Sisters*)

> **CONFLICT:** I love my boyfriend so much, but he's dead and having a difficult time trying to communicate with me from the afterlife because he's forced to use an unreliable medium with a criminal record: Whoopi Goldberg. (*Ghost*)

Conflicts keep your plot and your novel moving ahead because your character will be faced with decisions and come head-to-head with situations that will force her to either act or react. Spend some time weeding out the nonflicts in your own work. Or make these nonflicts into conflicts by raising the stakes for your character. What is at risk for your character if he does not get what he wants? What stands to be lost or gained? And, importantly, why will this choice matter to your protagonist, and, by extension, to your reader?

Assignment

The goal of today's assignment is to analyze the conflicts at work in your story. Are the stakes deep enough? Will these conflicts compel your characters to action? First, I want you to take a look at the synopsis you wrote for Day 3. Does your novel have, as Syd Field suggests, at least two major plot points, the first of which drives your character to action and the second of which is the turning point (or point of no return) for your character? Are the conflicts deep enough, important enough, or "big" enough to sustain the novel?

Now make a list of all the conflicts in your story. Can you locate any nonflicts, i.e., yearnings without action?

Finally, select the two biggest conflicts (what Syd Field would call Plot Point 1 and Plot Point 2, but what a novelist would term the rising conflict and the climax), and spend the rest of your time today writing each of these scenes. As your character deals with these conflicts, how does his personality/history/experiences/desires naturally cause him to act or react in this situation? Be sure to divide your time evenly between these scenes. As you get involved in a scene, it's easy to be tempted to keep working on it. But remember, this is still the prewriting stage. Your goal is to simply explore your ideas to be sure your conflicts are able to sustain a novel.

Once you've finished, assess what you've written. What is at stake for your character if he or she doesn't get what they want? How is the character changed by the conflict? Is the conflict internal or external? For now I'm only asking you to generally assess the conflicts in your story; however, you'll want to soon begin thinking about the narrative arc: the beginning, middle, and end of your story.

DAY 12: *Making the Most of Minor Characters*

By now, your novelistic world is populating itself with some interesting characters, and hopefully you've honed in on who your protagonist(s) will be. You've spent hours thinking about plot, conflicts, setting, and motivations. You've written bios, lists, and a handful of scenes, some which may be used, others that may be discarded. In other words, you've done a lot of work toward developing the larger schematics of your novel.

But remember, love is in the *details*. It's not too early to begin thinking about some of the finer details of the novel, and some of these details will come in the form of the minor characters who enter and exit your novel's world, sometimes without much of a sound. Minor characters are just that—minor. They do not have much onstage time, and more often than not, they make cameo appearances. Think again about all the people you've come into contact with today. These characters all had minor influences on you during your day, even if their sole purpose was to pour you a cup of coffee at breakfast. But how did you react to the individual pouring coffee? Were you annoyed at the slow service? Did you help her clean up the coffee she spilled on your table? Sure, you may never see that waitress again, but your interaction did reveal a snapshot of your own personality.

You've spent a good deal of time creating fully round characters in the previous days, and you know, of course, that your protagonist must evolve as the novel unfolds. However, not all of your characters need to be fully rounded. It's okay, in other words, for some of your characters to be flat or static characters; we don't need to know all characters' full histories, complexities, and desires. We don't even necessarily need to know how they've been affected by the various conflicts at work in your novel. However, each member of your cast of minor characters has a deeper significance within the novel itself: Each minor character must have a particular purpose, one that reveals some fundamental element about your main players.

Let's revisit our faithful example of *The Great Gatsby*. As you know, the main players were Jay Gatsby, Daisy, Tom Buchanan, and Nick Carraway, who is narrating the events of the story through his own eyes. Who are some of the minor characters, then? Think of Myrtle Wilson, Tom Buchanan's lover, or George Wilson, Myrtle's father. Think of Pammy, the daughter of Daisy and Tom. Think also of Meyer Wolfshiem, one of Gatsby's seedy old friends. Or Jordan Baker, Nick's sometime girlfriend. There are plenty of others, too. An entire cast of characters you may not have even considered, and some have larger roles than others. For instance, Myrtle is pivotal to the story's ending, though she's only ever granted a handful of scenes. Jordan Baker shows up for a few scenes, while poor, overlooked Pammy only graces the pages of the book for a few sentences. Blink and you might miss her. (And I'd be willing to wager a bet that many of you

who read *The Great Gatsby* a while ago forgot that Tom and Daisy even had a child.)

Regardless of the length of the stay, each of these minor characters functions specifically to reveal some personality trait or character aspect of a main player. Take, for instance, Pammy Buchanan, who is brought into her mother's luncheon to curtsy in her dress before Gatsby, Nick, and Jordan. During the brief visit, Daisy admits she only wanted to show off her daughter (a bit like a prized doll, one might imagine). And before we can say *Go East Egg*, she is rushed out of the scene by her nurse, the woman who usually cares for her. What does this brief encounter tell us about Daisy? How does Gatsby react? Does it reveal Daisy's innate nurturing and motherly instincts? Does it show Gatsby's affection toward the offspring of his eternal flame? Of course not; she's about as interested in her daughter as a flea is interested in a hairless guinea pig, which is to say, not a lot.

As you continue working toward your outline, begin to consider which minor characters might take the stage. It's a good idea to have at least some idea of their history, appearance, and personality, but it's essential to know their purpose within the confines of the novel. What will they reveal about the protagonist?

Assignment

The goal of the following assignment is to develop some of your minor characters. As your story line evolves, you'll likely find a need to expand your cast.

First, using the worksheet on page 107, come up with bios for at least ten potential minor characters. What kind of individuals will your protagonist encounter throughout the pages of the novel? You may want to consider relatives of your characters, coworkers, or classmates. Or you may wish to think about the various scene settings and the kind of people who might populate this scenery. For instance, if one scene is set in a park, will there be a hot-dog vendor? A street performer?

Next, spend the rest of your time writing several short scenes that involve minor characters. In what ways will these individuals react? How is your reader given a clearer picture about your protagonist? Remember, you can reveal much about your minor characters in a short space of time if you pay particular attention to details of appearance and/or how the characters carry themselves.

MINOR-CHARACTER BIO SHEET

Name: ....

Age: ....

Occupation:...
....

Brief physical description: ....
....

Brief history: ....
....
....

Relationship to main character(s):.............................
....
....

Purpose in the scene: ....
....
....

What does he/she reveal about main character(s)? ....
....
....

DAY 13: *Scene or Summary, or, Taking the Dull Parts Out*

Have you ever watched a movie or read a book that just felt, well, disjointed? Perhaps you felt it jumped from scene to scene, which confused you or maybe just annoyed you. This happens a lot in soap operas. Lauren and Jason are about to kiss when the scene cuts out, and suddenly you're in a darkened back alley with two thugs who are kidnapping Victor. Yikes!

Or maybe you are the type to get impatient when scenes are overly slow and long. "Do we really need all these details?" you might ask yourself as you flip pages, skimming to get to the "good stuff."

We've been writing in scene since Day 3—and we'll tackle the writing of your novel scene by scene—because a novel is simply a series of scenes strung together. However, without the necessary transitions and narrative summary, your novel is going to feel either like a.) a compilation of scenes and not a cohesive novel; or b.) an overly detailed story with a slow pace.

Narrative summary—which is essentially when the narrator summarizes some of the events of the story for the reader, without showing the scene directly—can serve two main purposes:

1. Orient your reader to changes in time, location, or point of view at the beginning of a scene.

2. Summarize what has happened so you can cut irrelevant, uninteresting, or unnecessary information.

The first purpose above is easy to understand; either between scenes or, more likely, as you begin each new scene, you're going to have to redirect your reader to changes that have taken place. If time has leapt forward, how much time? If you've changed locations, where is the reader now? If the POV character has flipped, how can you immediately alert your reader to this? That is, you don't have to show, in scene, how your character got from the end of chapter one to the beginning of chapter two by first, getting in a car, driving to the ferry, riding a ferry across the river, hopping in a taxi, and then walking the rest of the way. But you will have to make clear to the reader that these changes took place.

Alfred Hitchcock once wisely noted, "Drama is life with the dull parts taken out of it." If you've ever watched the hit television show *24*, have you noticed you never see the terrorist-fighting government agent, Jack Bauer, hit the john or retie his shoes or even eat three square meals a day? Of course not. There are too many other important things for Jack to be doing (for example, saving the world from nuclear bombs), and watching Jack tie his shoe would only serve to slow down the pace of the fast-action television show. The same holds true for our fictional worlds. If you find your story has "dull parts," you can simply choose to narrate these uneventful unfoldings in summary form. Narrative summary is like a black hole for dull parts, if you want to think of it that way.

Consider this brief moment from the start of a chapter in Michael Cunningham's *The Hours*: "She looks at the clock on the table. Almost two hours have passed....She takes a sip of cold coffee, and allows herself to read what she's written so far." Here, the author starts in scene: A fictional Virginia Woolf looks at the clock. Reads straightforward enough. But then Cunningham shifts to a line of summary: "Almost two hours have passed." Then, back to scene: Mrs. Woolf's coffee has gone cold.

Why did the author of this passage choose *not* to narrate the entire two hours that passed? Why weren't those two hours, hours Virginia Woolf spent in a writerly fugue state, put in scene, too? Consider Occam's razor: The simplest answer is usually the right one. Not much happened in those two hours worthy of narrating in a scene. Perhaps Mrs. Woolf refilled her inkwell or walked across the room to retrieve some more paper. Maybe she got a piece of lint in her eye, or heard her stomach growling. Did she ever have to get up to visit the "little ladies' room"? Maybe. But it's not important. Cunningham both alerts the reader to a time shift *and* cuts out the dull stuff by simply summarizing.

A masterful use of scene and narrative summary can really help you gain control of the pacing of your novel, too. Use summary when you want to speed up your narrative and scene when you want to slow down your story. And here, again, we can take a lesson from the movies. Directors provide more detail when they want to emphasize the importance of a scene—or make time appear to elapse more slowly. For example, think of Hilary Swank's final boxing scene in *Million Dollar Baby*. The viewer sees close-ups of the boxers, the sweat on Maggie's brow as she sizes up her opponent, the slow trickle of blood down her face, and the way her head hits the floor when she takes her final fall. This is an important moment, after all. Maggie's boxing career is ending before our eyes—so the director wants to draw attention to it.

Keep in mind that it's crucial to put your novel's most important moments in a scene to slow down time for your reader and detail crucial elements of your story; however, summary is useful, too, to quicken the pace and move forward in time. If scenes are the building blocks of your novel, summary is the glue that holds these blocks together.

Consider this example:

> When Luke shined his flashlight down to the bottom of the well, he could make out a body. The person's frame was small, so at first he thought it was a child or a teenager, but upon looking closer, he could see it was a woman. Her legs were bent at an awkward angle.
>
> "Hello down there?" Luke called. He could hear his voice echo off the stone walls of the well. "Hello?" At first he heard nothing, but then a slow moan rose like smoke out of the well.
>
> Luke knew he had to act fast. He put his flashlight down and turned to walk back to his blue Toyota pickup truck. He rifled in his pockets and found the silver key. When he turned the ignition, it started up smooth and easy. He backed out of the dirt parking lot and turned left on Round Bottom Road. He knew the police station was just about seven miles up on the right because he'd passed it on the way here. It would take fifteen minutes to get there. The trees were just turning red and orange all around him, so it looked like an explosion of color out of the corner of his eyes. Finally, he saw the police station, and he turned on his signal, eased his foot on the break, and made his turn. He wondered if that woman would be okay.

The above example begins in a scene: Luke is standing at a well when he discovers a body down below. However, the entire final paragraph could easily be provided in a quick summary in order to speed up the pace of the novel. What about: "Luke knew he had to act fast, so he rushed to his car and sped down the road to the police station." By providing summary, you avoid taking your reader through the sometimes tedious details that aren't necessary to your story. Plus, if Luke knew he had to act fast, would he really be noticing the autumn leaves on the trees? Not likely.

Assignment

The goal of today's writing is to practice using narrative summary within a scene. But, first, return to one of the scenes you wrote for either Day 10 or Day 11. Reread this scene and assess where you either are using or could use narrative summary. You might find it useful to print this scene and highlight with a marker. Next, ask yourself which details are not necessary to the scene—which details could you put in summary?

Now I'd like you to write the scene you imagine could follow this scene, chronologically, in your novel. However, I want you to either move forward significantly in time or change the setting in this new scene. Begin this scene with narrative summary before launching into the scene itself. Switch from narrative summary to scene narration at least twice in this section. Pay careful attention to what information can be summarized and what information should definitely be narrated in scene.

DAY 14: *Act One: The First Cluster of Scenes*

Today is the first day of the rest of your novel. Not that the work that's come before wasn't important. But today I want to focus on shaping your novel's timeline of events so you can begin the necessary steps toward outlining your novel. And, as you know, outlining will be an invaluable tool toward helping you conquer the ninety-day writing challenge. In such a short space of time, we don't have many days to waste! Hop to it.

As you know by now, you should be able to divide your novel, loosely, into three parts: a beginning, a middle, and an end. Some writers like to think of these as acts or as parts or as clusters. It's a fairly traditional model, and an excellent one for first-time novel writers. Essentially, each act is comprised of a series of scenes, and this cluster maintains a specific function within the arc of your novel. We'll be taking on the arc of your novel in further detail in a couple of weeks, but for now I want you to gain a general understanding of what each act of your novel can and should do.

But, first: Have you ever watched one of those incredibly cheesy reality dating shows, such as *The Bachelor*? I wouldn't recommend it. However, believe it or not, a show such as this one might provide us with some insights regarding Act One of your novel. In the first episode or so, the Bachelor is introduced to all the women who will be competing for his love. We learn about their histories and backstories; we learn about the bachelor himself, his trouble finding love, his hope that he'll meet his soul mate through the gonzo, accelerated journey created by reality television.

In the first episodes, the viewer is provided with introductions, stories, and brief interviews, and, as a result, we become invested in the contestants. We find ourselves rooting for Danica, from Nebraska, because she seems genuine and sweet, and we find ourselves rooting against Portia because she looks rather promiscuous in that emerald-green satin dress. Plus, she says "like" too much and is catty toward the other women.

We know that a main "plot point" of the bachelor will be the selecting of one (lucky?) bachelorette to ostensibly spend his life with in matrimony. In other words, the first episode or two is simply setup for the rest of the television series.

Act One of your novel, too, should serve as an introduction of your main characters, the "significant" or "starting point" event of your novel, and the overt or latent conflicts. By the end of Act One, the reader should know what drives your character: What is his history? What are his desires and motivation? Most importantly, what does your character want within the confines of this novel? In other words, what is at stake for your character in your novelistic world? What does he stand to gain if he attains his goals, and what will happen if he loses? Think about Romeo and Juliet. What Romeo wants most is Juliet. What is at stake if he can't have her? A colorless life, not worth living—so we learn toward the play's end.

By the end of the first act, your protagonist should be forced, coerced, or otherwise propelled to action; he must respond to the events that are unfolding before him.

In general, by the end of Act One, you should be able to answer these questions:

- What is the "significant event" of the novel?
- What is your character's motivation? What is at stake for her?
- Have you included enough scenes that provide the history and background for your character? In other words, have you developed your character enough in the first scenes for your reader to feel invested in her?
- Do you include scenes that either overtly show or hint at the challenges your character will face?
- Is the first third of your novel interesting enough to engage your reader and compel him to continue turning pages?

Often, when authors query editors or agents, they are asked to send only the first fifty or so pages. The logic here is that if the first fifty pages don't sustain the attention of a reader, the second hundred and fifty pages likely won't either.

Assignment

The goal of today's work is to begin brainstorming some likely plot points and scenes for inclusion in the first third of your novel/novel outline.

First, I want you to come up with a list of twenty first lines of your novel. Each should be different, and each should immediately grab the attention of your reader. A first line that reveals conflict or tension immediately is often a good lead in to your story. Don't focus too much on perfection at this point: Just brainstorm the various (and interesting) ways you can enter your story.

Next, write a list of at least five different scenes (and their summaries) that may be included in the first act. You may wish to review the questions above when you draw up this list of scenes.

Finally, write at least one of the scenes from your list above. We're not quite to the outline yet—so feel free to explore this character and this scene to see where it will take you.

DAY 15: *Act Two: The Second Cluster of Scenes*

Let's continue exploring *The Bachelor* again, for the sake of our learning. (And not for the sake of guilty-pleasure television consumption.) The "middle" episodes are really the heart and backbone of the series. These episodes include the drama, the tears, the pleading, and the backstabbing; in other words, these episodes include the conflict. We learn that the bachelor and Kelcey kissed in the hot tub, but then he learned that Kelcey had a boyfriend back home. Danica reveals that she is actually a mother of a one-month-old son, whom she left at home to come on the show in hopes of pursuing her Hollywood dreams. In essence, Act Two is your story.

In Act Two, you're going to have to put your characters into some hot water (the metaphorical kind, not the literal kind that the bachelor and Kelcey were splashing around in). You're going to have to create conflict and increase the yearning of your characters. Act Two of your novel is the realm of conflict. This portion of your novel should be dedicated to deepening the conflict and heightening the drama; it should be where "bad things happen" to your characters, even to your good characters, and especially to characters you like. Remember, yearning drives plot. Conflict, conflict, conflict. This may be difficult for some of us who, in our real lives (i.e., away from the writing table), are conflict adverse. We strive to stay out of trouble and to make decisions to bring us as close as possible to our desired outcomes. We are nonconfrontational, unless seriously provoked. And in this particular way, fiction does not mirror real life. In fiction we work to create tension; in life we strive to ease it.

By the end of Act Two, you should be able to answer these questions:

- Where have you deepened the drama?
- Where have you added complications for your protagonist?
- How are my character's motivations, desires, and values causing him to react to events and situations in a way particular to him?
- How is my character changing? How is he affected by the events unfolding before him?

- What is the climax of my novel? The key moment for my protagonist's understanding of self?

Assignment

The goal of today is to begin envisioning the middle section of your novel. Hopefully by now you're beginning to see how your novel might be shaped with character, plot, and conflict. You've spent two weeks developing your story and brainstorming methods for deepening the conflict and heightening the drama.

First, take out a piece of paper and draw a timeline of events that have taken place in Act One through Act Two. This timeline need not be fancy—a simple straight line with tick marks will do. Plot all the points you've listed in yesterday's exercise and continue plotting points until you run out of ideas.

Next, come up with a synopsis of Act Two, using the timeline you just drew. You can either write this synopsis in paragraph form, or you may wish to bullet point a list of scenes, along with their respective summaries. Consider where you ended your list of scenes yesterday. What steps will your character have to take in order to get from point A (the end of Act One) to point B (the climax)? Try your best to imagine each scene individually.

Next, write one of these scenes. Try not to be too rigid in your expectations of the scene. Instead let it naturally evolve and see to which interesting places it might take you.

DAY 16: *Act Three: The Final Cluster of Scenes*

The bachelor has once again found himself in a mess. He's developed real feelings for Danica and Portia. And in a surprise twist, Kelcey really opened up to him about her history and her feelings during their alone time, and now he's torn between three women.

The final episodes, however, find the bachelor resolving the complications that have faced him. He realizes he needs someone who will be both his best friend and his soul mate. He realizes he wants someone who will get along with his family, not just someone who will canoodle with him in the hot tub. He's changed, the show leads us to believe, and while he was flighty before (he has, after all dated twenty-five women in six weeks!), now he knows exactly who he wants to spend his life with. The journey, his journey, *our* journey, frankly, has come to the journey's end. And the final rose goes to…

In the final third of your novel, you should be working toward resolving the conflicts and problems your character faced in Act Two of your novel. In this final section, we learn the consequences for your character. He could either:

a.) Get what he wants.
b.) Not get what he wants.
c.) Get what he wants but realize it is no longer important to him.
d.) Not get what he wants, but get something that is even better than what he wanted in the first place.

The threads of your plot must come together in the final scenes, and you'll need to tie up any loose ends. Ultimately, we'll need to know how your character changed from the beginning of the novel to the end.

By the end of the final act, you should be able to answer the following:

- How has my character changed since the start of the novel?
- Have I resolved all plot points?
- What has my character learned? What were the consequences of the novel?
- What does my character want for the future? (Beyond the novel's pages, even?)
- Is my final scene strong enough? Poignant enough?

Assignment

Today's goal will be to begin thinking about what kind of scenes will be involved in the final act of your novel.

First, return to your timeline from yesterday and continue filling in the plot points. Then come up with a synopsis of Act Three, using the timeline you just drew. You can either write this synopsis in paragraph form, or you may wish to bullet point a list of scenes, along with their respective summaries. Consider where you ended your list of scenes yesterday. What steps will your character need to take in order to get from point A (the end of Act Two) to point B (the final resolution)? What kind of ending do you imagine for your novel? Try your best to imagine each scene individually.

Next, write twenty novel-ending lines. This is the last line the reader reads (obviously), so it needs to be a good one and encapsulate the final tone of the novel.

Finally, write one of the scenes from Act Three. Try not to have too many expectations of the scene. In other words, as you are writing, you may discover that in the end, the character does not get what he wants after all.

For the past two weeks, you've done a lot of thinking and writing toward the characters, plot, setting, and conflicts of your novel. The past few days, we began addressing the fundamentals of the arc of your story. However, as you're well aware, some of the necessary scenes and information will have already taken place prior to the "present" of your novel, or where your novel actually starts.

Each novel is narrated from a specific point in time, from point A to point B. In the case of *The Great Gatsby*, the present time of the narrative is from Jay Gatsby's arrival into West Egg until shortly after his untimely death several months later. However, this book also affords us several glimpses into the past—into events that happened before the novel's narrated time began. And this backstory, as you know by now, will become vital to the progressing events of the novel. After all, it is Gatsby's unfaltering love (or is it an obsession?) for Daisy, their past love connection back in Louisville, Kentucky, that drives his unrelenting quest to buy ... er, win ... Daisy's love again. We have to know a bit about the past in order for the events of the novel to fully resonate with the reader.

Most novels will likely find themselves flashing back to an earlier time to reveal aspects of a character's history or experiences. But before you get flashback slaphappy, you should learn some key rules:

1. Once you've decided on a starting point for your novel's narration, you should do your best to maintain narrating the present story.

2. Flashing back too often or for too long can confuse your reader. If you find the need to continually flash-

back to explain your character's behaviors or desires, your story should probably begin earlier. For example, if you find your protagonist, Zane, was deeply affected by his time in war, and you keep flashing back to scenes of battle, maybe you should simply start the novel with Zane hunkered down in a bunker, fighting off enemy fire.

3. You often can use narrative summary, instead of an entire scene, to convey the necessary backstory. Executed artfully, a reader won't realize that she is being shifted back and forth in time. Consider this example:

> Leonard felt his fingers go cold and his face grow hot. He couldn't believe Tapanga's words as she said goodbye. He felt like he had a rock lodged in his throat. He thought back to what his mother had told him over and over as a child, sometimes screaming in his face when he did something wrong: *No one will ever love you. You are unlovable.* Deflated now, Leonard thought that maybe his mother was right.

In this brief snippet of a flashback, we sense the connection of the past to the emotions of the present. In other words, we know Leonard feels so emotionally fragile in the present moment because of the quick snapshot of his abusive mother. However, this flashback was brief and quick, keeping the reader's attention focused on the story being narrated.

Flashing back can be extraordinarily useful when conveying emotions or trying to explain the actions, motivations, or desires of your characters. However, flashing back too often can feel disorienting and unnecessary. You'll want to use flashback economically, so make every memory a significant one.

The goal of today's assignment is to practice using flashback within your scenes. First, I'd like to write a stand-alone scene of flashback from the point of view of your protagonist that takes place prior to any events of your novel. Perhaps this scene of flashback could take place in the protagonist's childhood or young adult years. Put this scene away. Next, write a scene in the "present moment" of your novel, trying your best to incorporate, from memory, the important details from the flashback scene you just wrote. The trick will be to include the flashback without having it overwhelm the present scene.

Next, select two to three scenes you've already written for a previous exercise. Revise these scenes, adding sentences or paragraphs of flashback to deepen emotions or explain the motivations of your character.

DAY 18: *Don't Be Tone-Deaf*

Tone can be a tricky concept to discuss because it doesn't involve any concrete element of fiction, per se. In effect, the tone of your novel, or of an individual scene within your novel, describes the mood it evokes, or the overall feel. And just how do you talk about something you can feel, but you can't see? Though difficult, it is possible. And perhaps this is why poets and musicians have spent hundreds of years exploring an intangible concept such as love.

One reason tone is a difficult concept to explore is because it comes from a variety of sources within your work. First, the tone will be part and parcel of the narrator or your POV character. What is his or her overall purpose in telling the novel? Is this story a coming-of-age novel? A mystery? A cathartic release of some sort? A romance? And how would you describe the temperament of your narrator? Is she nervous? Anxious? Moody? Uncertain? Pompous? Happy? Naive? Bombastic? Whoever is narrating the story, remember, will have the greatest impact on exactly how that story gets told.

Consider, briefly, the following example, taken from the first pages of Nabokov's haunting novel, *Lolita*:

> Lolita, light of my life, fire of my loins. My sin, my soul. Lo-lee-ta: the tip of the tongue taking a trip of three steps down the palate to tap, at three, on the teeth. Lo. Lee. Ta. She was Lo, plain Lo, in the morning, standing four feet ten in one stocking. She was Lola in slacks. She was Dolly at school. She was Dolores on the dotted line. But in my arms she was always Lolita.

In these few short sentences, the narrator Humbert Humbert not only describes young Lolita, but allows us a glimpse into the tone of the novel. In this passage, we know Lolita's approximate height; we know she is a school-age girl; we know she is Humbert Humbert's lover. Yet the *way* the narrator provides this description—particularly through his creepy repetition of her name—reveals his deep and abiding obsession with her. From the onset of this novel the reader knows this romance won't be a normal one, and once dear Humbert Humbert's age is revealed, the obsessive tone of the opening fits the character. Yet, there is a musicality and lightness to the tone, too—*Lo, Lee, Ta,* like the notes of a scale. And perhaps it is this lightness that convinces us, the readers, to continue reading such a sordid tale.

Tone also stems from other decisions that you, the writer, are making in terms of word choice, imagery, and setting. You might recall our explorations of settings a couple of weeks ago, wherein we discussed that the setting can be used to reveal the tone of the scene or the mood of the character. For example, you'll find it much more difficult to evoke an ominous tone on a bright and crisp spring morning, as the sun is just peeking out of the sky. Imagery, too, will become essential toward conveying tone. For instance, chirping birds don't necessarily convey a menacing tone. Unless, that is, the birds are numerous, black, and hyper-aggressive, as in Alfred Hitchcock's film *The Birds.*

But filmmakers have an easier time conveying tone to their viewers. In films, tone is often set by the addition of a musical soundtrack. I'm sure you can recall the high-pitched, repetitive, screeching music in the American thriller classic *Psycho.* This chaotic music is directly related to the character in the scene—a knife-wielding maniac, Norman Bates.

Think for a moment of the novel you're shaping so far—what kind of tone do you think you've created throughout? Before continuing, take a look at the last couple of scenes you've written. What one-word adjective would you use to describe the tone? If this scene were made into a film, which song do you think you'd use in the soundtrack? These questions might seem like simple ones, but if the tone of the scene does not match the content of the scene, the writing can feel a bit stilted.

More often than not, if you're paying close attention to developing your characters and, as result, your voice, the

tone of your scene will naturally evolve. However, it's crucial you keep tone in mind as you're making some crucial choices about diction, imagery, and setting. How do you want your characters to feel?

Assignment

The goal of this assignment is to explore in further depth the tone of your novel and how it is affected by character, imagery, and word choice.

To warm up, I want you to simply brainstorm a list of words—adjectives, nouns, and verbs—that you associate with the following descriptors. Really stretch your imagination as you try to come up with as many associative words as possible to tonally convey the feeling evoked when you hear these expressions.

Ominous

Upbeat

Quirky

Manipulative

Mysterious

Obsessive

Next, select a scene, any scene, that you've written in the last two weeks, and print it out. I'd like you to assess the tone of this scene by circling any word that is evocative of the tone. Highlight any images or description of setting that work toward conveying tone, and then write at the bottom of the page a three-sentence description of the scene's tone *and* how it relates to the POV character and his mind-set. Next, select a song for the "soundtrack" of this scene. (That is, if this scene were made into a movie, which song would fit better—"Don't Stop Believin' " or "Endless Love"?

Finally, write two short scenes involving your main protagonist "discovering" something, each with a different intentional tone. So, for instance, if the tone in one scene is light (as the protagonist finds a winning lottery ticket), the other could be dark (as he discovers that his father illegally rigged the lotto numbers and killed a lottery representative in the process). In each, use at least one symbolic image to represent the tone of the scene (think of Hitchcock's *The Birds*).

DAY 19: *Novel Synopsis, the Preblueprint*

You are three writing days away from completing a sturdy outline of your novel, and you should be proud of yourself. It takes faith in your ideas, patience, and, well, a little bit of guts to spend nearly three weeks developing and prewriting your novel. But the reward will be worth it. When you finally start the linear writing of your novel, the process will go much more smoothly if you have the blueprint in hand. But let's face it, it'll still be work.

Unlike many of the other days' assignments, today we won't focus on a specific element of fiction writing; instead we'll focus on drawing up a detailed synopsis of your novel. Novelists who query agents and editors will likely find they are asked to first submit a synopsis of their work. Based on whether or not the agent found the synopsis compelling and well written, you'll be asked to send in a copy of your manuscript.

Writing a synopsis is useful for several reasons. First, it allows you to put down on paper (or computer screen) the plot of your novel in paragraph form, along with other necessary details of character, conflict, and setting. A syn-

opsis is an excellent way for you to organize your thoughts, plot points, and story line prior to writing your outline.

A good synopsis should mimic the voice and tone of your novel. One of the biggest mistakes writers make when crafting a synopsis is creating one that's boring. Your novel is complex, intricate, and narrated using a particular voice, as your synopsis should be. If your novel is exciting, your synopsis should be, too. If your novel is fast paced, ditto your synopsis. If your novel is a slow-moving intricate portrait of the interior life of your character, yep, your synopsis should reflect this.

Your synopsis should also contain the right amount of backstory to properly orient your reader. What does your reader need to know about your protagonist before he or she is able to understand the context of the story? In writing the synopsis, you'll need to be mindful of your reader every step of the way. You, the author, will be telling a story: the story of your novel. What's the best way to hook your reader? What details can you reveal that are interesting, intriguing, or compelling? Remember, sometimes your synopsis is the only shot you've got at convincing an agent or editor to review your work.

The shape, or arc, of your synopsis, too, should mimic your novel. You'll want to add the necessary details to introduce your character; you'll need to include the motivations and yearnings of your protagonist; you'll have to include the necessary details surrounding the climax scene—the most important moment in your novel's story line, and certainly a defining moment of decision and/or clarity for your character—and why it's crucial to your story. And, finally, although it might feel counterintuitive to "give away" the ending of your story, you'll need to explain how your story gets resolved.

You may know some of these things already—or you may not. But as you're writing your synopsis, you should fill in as many of the fine details as you can. Your synopsis, if fully drawn, will assist you enormously in the production of your outline, which will be our next task.

Assignment

Today's assignment is straightforward, and if you've done your requisite writing assignments up to this point, you may find this assignment easier than expected. Write a synopsis of your novel, including as much detail as possible. Editors and agents often ask for a long synopsis of your novel, which can be anywhere from eight to ten pages. What are the most important details that a blind reader would need to know about your story? What minor details can you leave out? What backstory will you need to give your reader so as to orient him?

DAYS 20 AND 21: *Ladies and Gentlemen ... the OUTLINE!*

Congratulations! If you've come this far in your ninety-day writing challenge, you should be extraordinarily pleased with yourself. Heck, you should throw a party (but maybe just a small one where you are the only person in attendance.) You've come a long way in nearly three weeks: You've spent a couple of hours a day doing something you always wanted to do: working on a novel. Of course, this is only the beginning of the process. (Thus, the *small* party intended only for yourself.)

What you've done so far is lay the groundwork for your novel's blueprint. As discussed throughout this book, you'll need a sturdy outline to be able to produce the necessary pages in the seventy days that remain. Your outline will ensure that you stay on task, that you've considered the conflicts and consequences for your characters, and that you've done some research on your characters' histories or the time period in which your novel is set. I'd be willing to bet that your novel idea has morphed quite a bit from Day 1 to Day 19 when you wrote your synopsis. You've probably created characters you never would have considered, explored possible plotlines, and delved into pockets of your creativity you didn't even know existed. Perhaps you began this challenge thinking you wanted to write about a World War II nurse, but now you've decided to write about the granddaughter of the nurse, who plays in a fledgling country band called the Florence Nightingales, a band that busks for money on the streets of downtown Tupelo. This, you think to yourself, is a much more compelling story to write. And if you've done the necessary exploratory and developmental work, you're probably right.

Days 20 and 21 will be dedicated to constructing your outline, scene by scene, and, luckily, you've already accomplished much of the work. Consider the work you did on Days 14, 15, and 16, when you were asked to think about the three acts, or parts, of your novel. Consider also how you can break down the synopsis from Day 19 into compartments or scenes.

As you recall in a previous chapter on outlining techniques, it's important to find the method that meshes best with your writing process. Do you tend to write by hand first and then type up what you've written? Do you type directly into a word-processing program? Are you one of the few, like fiction writer Richard Powers, who uses voice recognition software to dictate your work? If so, which outlining technique do you think will work best? Are you a more tactile learner? Would you benefit from a physical flowchart you could tape to the wall next to your desk?

Regardless of the style you choose, you'll need to spend these next two days mapping out your novel, scene by scene. While this may seem like a tedious process—maybe you've been dreading these days all along!—the work you do now will save you valuable time and energy at a later date. And what will you do with all this saved time and energy? You'll write, of course!

Assignment

Quickly skim through all your exercises from Day 1 through Day 19, paying particular attention to Days 14, 15, 16, and 19. Chances are that by this point you've already come up with most of the conceptual material for your book.

Now, you guessed it: Outline your novel, scene by scene, providing as much detail for each scene as possible. Be sure that you note, *at a minimum*, the setting, characters, and conflict/plot of each scene. You'll also want to note how each scene is resolved, even if that resolution is a cliff-hanger. This assignment will likely take you a while to accomplish, and DO NOT SKIP THIS ASSIGNMENT under the false assumption that you've already done this developmental work in the synopsis and previous lessons. Breaking your novel into discrete scenes will prove absolutely crucial for later lessons as we work through your novel one scene at a time. Now get to work! You've got a novel to write, after all, and fewer than seventy days to do it!

The rest of 90 Days to Your Novel is divided by week, and each week contains several assignments. Be sure to allott enough time every week—still roughly two to three hours a day—to complete all assignments. Some assignments may take you more time than others.

FIRST ASSESSMENTS

*I*nhale. Exhale. Inhale. Exhale. You may want to stretch those writing fingers or do a few deep-knee bends for good measure. You've been doing a lot of writing these past few weeks, and maybe all this sitting has taken a physical toll. You've skipped the gym or your morning walk a few times in order to squeeze in your writing hours. Or maybe you ate a TV dinner at your desk while typing away. Writers are notorious for having digestive disorders. Has your spouse/partner/friend/kids complained yet that you're not spending enough time with them? Nobody said writing would be easy. Nobody said writing would help your social life either. So go ahead and stretch out your legs and back; take a few inhales and exhales. Now, at-ten-TION! That's about all the break time you have. Back to work. You've got a novel to write, and only sixty-odd days to do it.

As discussed earlier, the key to successful novel writing, like any large-scale project, is to break the seemingly daunting task into smaller, more manageable segments. You, of course, just spent the last three weeks doing that. And now, as luck would have it (though luck really didn't have anything to do with it), you are the proud new parent of an outline. Make no mistake about it, this outline will become the most important tool for you as you progress throughout this ninety-day writing challenge. Perhaps it sounds a bit hokey to you, but you really should be proud of yourself. In three short weeks you managed to take your novel idea and turn it into a fully functioning blueprint for your novel-to-be. That's quite an accomplishment, if you ask me, more than many would-be novelists do in their lifetimes. You've already created some separation between yourself and ninety percent of the wannabes. Hopefully, you've surprised yourself a little bit with your ability to stick to a schedule (when prodded), with your ability to sustain your writing and fill up your notebook or your computer screen, and with your new and improved dedication to writing. That'll be the trick to writing a novel in ninety days, after all: producing pages.

By this point, not only have you drafted a working outline of your novel, you've also begun to develop the necessary writing habits that will help you see this project through. And these habits will become just as important as the outline itself. After all, what good is a blueprint if you don't have the proper building materials? The blueprint, then, becomes just another drawing of another house. If you've come this far and don't think you can make it, that's fine. But then you can no longer say you want to write a novel. That's a bit like saying you want to go deep-sea fishing, but you don't want to get on the boat. Or you want to win a marathon, but you don't want to run it. Sure, we all want glory without any of the work.

For those of you who are hungry and eager to sink your teeth into your writing project, tackling that book scene by scene, let's get to it. I'm glad you find the work is worth it. You've begun to establish and develop your characters, you've practiced scene writing, and you have a good sense of where your novel will begin and end. Heck, you've prac-tically written the thing in your mind already. So the next step will be writing the novel, right?

Wrong.

But close. This week, instead, we want to pay particular attention to your outline, to the narrative arc of your story, and to some of the other finer details that might trip you up along the way as you write. That is, I want you to be as prepared as possible when you begin writing your novel so you can spend your daily writing hours freed up from the logistical concerns of your story line. This *freeing up* will allow you the luxury of truly getting lost in your novelistic world, as you won't have to continually ask yourself which way your characters might turn next, what the next plot point will be, or if you've built up enough tension leading to the climax of your novel. If you already *know* these ele-ments of your story, you can refocus on the most impor-tant aspects of your work: developing a compelling story and creating characters your readers truly care about. In the end, character and story are the two most important features of any novel.

Before you read further, I'd like for you to print out a hard copy of your outline, or, if you've handwritten it on paper or note cards, I'd like you to set them in front of you. You'll need to spend some time reading it, assessing it, and thinking about the various uses for the individual scenes you've charted for your novel.

WEEK 4, ASSIGNMENT 1: *Assessing Scene Worth*

Not all scenes are created equal. Each scene serves to reveal only a snapshot of the entire picture. Or, to borrow from William Blake, only one "grain of sand" on the beach that is your novel. As discussed in the chapter on scene structure, each scene must have a specific purpose within the context of your novel, and this purpose should be clear to you as you are writing. Your readers will expect each scene to contribute in some way to either the plot or the character development, and if your scenes feel directionless or, even worse, pointless, your reader might just put down the novel altogether and never pick it up again. Nothing is more frustrating than feeling like you've wasted time reading a book with no point. With each scene that has materialized on your outline, you should be able to answer the following questions:

- What is the purpose of this scene?
- How is this scene related to the scene immediately before/after?
- What characters are involved in this scene?
- What is the setting?
- What is at stake for the protagonist in this scene?
- What is the conflict in this scene?
- How does this scene further develop my novel's plot?

If, as you peruse your outline, you're unable to come up with a clear intention of a given scene, you might be wiser to cut that scene, combine it with another, or redevelop it. In these early stages, don't be afraid to cut scenes you don't feel contribute to your holistic vision of the novel. Remember, each dead-end street you drive down during the next sixty-odd days will waste your valuable time as you turn around and get to your final destination.

At this point, I want you to number each scene on your outline. There is no right or wrong number of scenes to have—some novels have as many scenes as they have chapters. In other novels, some chapters are comprised of several scenes cobbled together. After you've numbered each scene, and on a separate piece of paper (or in a separate document, if you are working on your computer), I want you to answer each question from page 135. To be clear, this process will involve some time as you mull over the decisions you made last week. But be warned: Do not take shortcuts by answering the questions in your head. You'll need to actually articulate, on paper, the answers to these questions: Why? (As my mother would say to me as a child, "Why are you always asking why?") Because when you force yourself to verbalize the purpose and intent of each scene, you'll have a clearer sense of whether that scene is working and whether that scene is even relevant to your novel. A scene you originally thought was crucial to your character development may wind up too similar to a different scene, and is therefore unnecessary. For instance, if you note that the purpose of scene 10 and scene 12 both work to reveal your protagonist's fear of rejection due to the fact that he was born with six fingers on each hand, you might want to simply combine those scenes into one. Trust that your readers are astute enough to pick up on this insecurity the first time you wrote it.

WEEK 4, ASSIGNMENT 2: *Assessing Scene Variety*
You've heard the cliché: Variety is the spice of life. We use clichés in real life—though never in fiction—because sometimes they hold a kernel of truth. (See what I did there? I used a cliché to demonstrate my point.) Few people can stand the monotony of facing the same thing over and over and over and over and over and over again. The same holds true in fiction; you must afford your reader a variety of scene types;

otherwise they'll likely grow bored. You'll need to include an artful balance of both internal and external scenes in order to maintain a good pace in your novel, thus sustaining the interest of your reader. If every scene is one of interior monologue, your reader will probably tune out. However, if every scene contains only dialogue or action, your reader may never truly know the interiority of your main character, and therefore your reader won't connect with him. If you need to brush up on the types of internal and external scenes, you may want to review the scene types presented in a previous chapter before continuing this assignment.

Seems like just yesterday you started your novel. Stretch your memory back to the very first assignment on Day 1: Ready, Set, Go (With What You Know)(see page 49). If you can't remember this assignment, get it out, print it out, or pull it up on your computer where you saved it. In this assignment you were asked to brainstorm a list of your memories—the people, places, and things you surrounded yourself with as a child. Now, for just a few moments, I want you to add three more categories. Favorite Moments, Biggest Fears, Biggest Upsets, and Most Embarrassing Moments. Spend about ten minutes brainstorming these categories on a separate piece of paper before reading on. Don't worry; I'll wait.

A good notion to keep in mind is that fiction is a mirror held up to our own lives. Review the list you just brainstormed. Are your experiences, fears, and traumas more internal or external? For example, does your biggest upset stem from a car accident (external) or from your sensitivity after the death of your family dog, Pepper (internal)? What do you fear most? Failure (internal) or the possibility that your hair will catch on fire (external)? Was your favorite moment when you accomplished a personal goal (internal) or when you purchased your first home (external)?

If you prefer to think of novel writing in metaphorical terms again, here's another one: Your novel is a football game, and each scene is a play that allows you to gain some yards. Each scene should function to reveal an element of character or plot that will be vital to your novel as a whole. But the quarterback can't keep calling the same play over and over again. No, that would grow predictable to the defense, and therefore not many yards would be gained. The quarterback has to call a different play each time in order to keep the defense on their toes and, ultimately, in order to score a touchdown. The same holds true for your novel: Each scene should reveal a snapshot of the entire picture, but, as you know from your own brainstorm list, this will require your protagonist to experience the world on both an internal and an external level—and in different ways. You'll need scenes that reveal the interior depth of your character, and you'll need scenes that put your character into the center of the action. In some scenes your character will be alone, which will require you to master the art of indirect speech. In other scenes, you'll need to place your characters in dialogue with other characters so we know how they think and how they speak. In other words, you need scene variety.

Have you ever read a novel that felt slow to you in some spots? Have you ever read a novel where it took too long for something to happen? Or have you ever come to a boring section of a novel and started to skim until you got to a "good part" again? The problem with many of these novels is that the pacing is off. Perhaps too many internal scenes were positioned back to back, or perhaps the drama felt unearned because you didn't know what the characters were thinking. (This can often be the result of too many action scenes in a row.) Think for a moment about the kinds of scenes that cause you to lose interest in a novel, and keep this in mind as you write. Don't write the kinds of scenes that bore you; otherwise you're simply passing the baton of boredom to someone else. And that's not very nice, now, is it?

It's never too early to start thinking about the pacing of your novel. In fact, if you address the issue of pacing and scene variety before you write your novel, the problems you find as you write will be much easier to remedy. It becomes time-consuming to eliminate or reorder scenes after you've written your entire book, because for each scene you cut or reorder, you'll discover several loose ends that need to be fixed as well. And, as you know, with only a ninety-day schedule, time is not something you want to waste.

Before moving on to the next section, take out your outline and find yourself a highlighter. For all the scenes on your outline—you've numbered them by now—I want you to label whether you think an internal or an external scene will be necessary. Simply place an *I* for internal or an *E* for external next to the individual scenes on your outline. Now ask yourself:

- Are the internal and external scenes in a healthy balance with one another? Are there any sections of your novel that contain too many back-to-back external scenes, such as dialogue scenes, dramatic scenes, action scenes, or, conversely, too many internal scenes, setting-forward scenes (ones that rely heavily on setting to reveal the character or tone), emotional scenes, interior monologue scenes?

- Are there any places in your outline where you are concerned with losing the reader's interest? What do you think is the slowest part of your novel?

- Are there any portions of your outline that could include an internal scene in order to reveal the thoughts, fears, or motivations behind your main character's actions?

You may find that, as luck would have it, your outline is balanced in perfect harmony. Or, if you are one of the 99.9 percent of people who need to make a few adjustments to your outline, now is the time to do so. How can you rearrange, cut, or reenvision your scene order or scene types to keep an even pace in your novel? You may find you can squeeze a short internal scene between two dramatic/action scenes. Or you may find you can eliminate too many internal scenes altogether. Be sure to spend the necessary time assessing scene variety at this point. You'll be thankful that you did.

WEEK 4, ASSIGNMENT 3: *Assessing the Narrative Arc*
In the last assignment, you were asked to pay some attention to the pacing of your novel through scene variety. However, pacing is also achieved by giving your novel a natural narrative arc. As we discussed in an earlier assignment, the arc of your novel is, quite simply, how your novel progresses from the beginning, into the stakes-raising middle, and then finally to the end.

Have you ever played that amusement-park game where you roll a bowling ball on a metal track with two humps? The goal of this game is to roll the ball hard enough to get the ball over the first hump, but not too hard so that the bowling ball flies over the second one. The aim of the player is to balance the ball in the small valley between the two humps in the track. The trick to this game—and it's difficult, trust me!—is to give the ball enough momentum, but not too much.

Your novel functions much in this way, too. You want your novel to have the necessary momentum to keep your reader turning the pages, but you don't want to give away too much information, detail, or plot points too quickly. If your reader feels she already knows what's going to happen, she'll likely put down your book and look for another form of entertainment. I hear lawn darts are making a comeback.

As we discussed in the assignment from Days 14, 15, and 16, a novel can be loosely divided into three parts, or acts, as we'll be calling them, and each of these acts has a different function within the context of your novel. In this assignment, I want to pay particular attention to your novel's three acts to ensure your story line builds, heightens, deepens, and resolves itself at the right pace.

But, first, I want you to return to your outline again. Before we move on, and on a separate piece of paper, I want you to make a list of all the ways in which your character's yearning is blocked in your outline, as it stands now. Again, you must make a physical list, not just a mental one. Why? Because the way we process information in our heads and on paper is quite different, and the reader never has the advantage of being in your head. Go on, then, write down your list. Take your time with it. I'm in no hurry.

Once you have finished, ask yourself: Have you drawn out the yearning or the conflict long enough to sustain the novel? Does each scene in your outline offer a glimpse into your protagonist's yearning and the ways in which it is being blocked?

Remember from our earlier lessons: Yearning generates plot. Without some thwarted desires, your novel will likely go nowhere. What fun is it to read a novel about a character who always gets her way? It would read something like this:

> Mary is a beautiful, fit, energetic woman with two gorgeous children who lives in a large Colonial house on the cul-de-sac of a pleasant suburb, along with a handsome husband who makes gobs of money and can afford to buy her anything she wants. The husband and wife live pleasantly together, whiling away their hours on good conversation, lively entertainment from their darling children, and, of course, their deepening love for one another.

A reader's reaction, if he were kind, might be: zzzzzzzzzz. Boring. Welcome to Snoozeville. Population: Anyone who has bothered to read this devastatingly boring paragraph. Remember, do not, not under any circumstance, even if you really, really want to, give your characters what they want. (See the sticky note you placed near your writing desk.) At least, not right away. Holding back on giving your characters what they want is a surefire way to create the tension and inner conflict necessary to propel your plot forward. So, perhaps Mary has those two beautiful children, that gorgeous house, and a husband who often comes home late smelling of booze and cheap perfume. Suddenly, Mary seems more sympathetic; she's a woman scorned, and there is plenty of room for your plot to grow.

If your list of the ways in which your character's yearning is thwarted or blocked is brief or paltry, you're going to have to find ways to deepen the conflict in your novel. What kinds of scenes can you include? What might stand in the way of what your character wants? Is the yearning generated in your outline enough to sustain a novel-length work?

Next, with a copy of your completed outline in front of you, I'd like for you to draw a line roughly one-third of the way through it. Also, draw a line two-thirds of the way down. (If you are using note cards, simply include a blank divider between cards to separate your outline into thirds.) What you've done is roughly divide your outline into three parts, coinciding with—let's hope—your novel's three acts.

In this assignment, you'll need to spend some time critically assessing each of these three parts of your novel. Remember the distinctions between Acts One, Two, and Three that we explored in Days 14–16? You have a story to tell, and you have 80,000 words or so in which to do it. You don't want to give information away too quickly; otherwise, your reader will have no incentive to keep reading. Where can you add a scene to build tension and yearning? Where can you delete a scene that is giving away too much, too quickly? Remember, you're better off deleting nonessential scenes so you don't waste time writing them out.

Act One

Do you remember back in the days of your English composition classes when you learned that a good essay begins with a hook? The hook was a particularly compelling line or fact or statistic or famous quote that immediately grabbed the attention of your reader. While the hook of a novel works differently than the hook of an essay, the general concept is the same. You need to convince your reader that your novel is worth reading, and you do this by immediately capturing his or her interest. The best way to immerse your reader in the novel is to start the first scene in *medias res*, which translates to "in the middle of things." When you start your novel with action, your reader will feel like she has to keep reading in order to catch up, or she might miss the train altogether. Your novel should start at a significant moment in relation to the plot and the character. Don't just start at any random moment. Really think about why you are choosing to begin where you do. For instance, have your key protagonists Kirk and Amber just married? Is the wedding or their marriage a significant part of the story or related to the plot? Well, that depends on the story you're narrating, of course. The wedding might be an excellent starting point if you're writing a classic caper novel about their adventures during a honeymoon in Morocco. However, this might not be the right place to start if the novel doesn't have much to do with the relationship between Amber and Nick in the first place, and instead follows Amber's relationship with her adoptive mother.

Act One must also include the "why should I care about this" element. One of your main goals in Act One is to get your reader to care about your character. How is she sympathetic? How is she flawed? What does your character want? And what is at stake for him if he doesn't get what he wants? You should skim your outline to make sure you've provided enough information about the history, desires, motivations, and fears of your main characters.

By the end of the first act, something has to happen. That is, your character must be faced with a conflict that either forces or compels him to action. If by the end of your first act, you still find that nothing has happened that is of great import to your character or your plot, you'll need to remedy this.

Take a look at the first third of your outline and ask yourself the following questions:

- Does my novel start in the right place? What is the significance of the moment in which my novel starts?
- Does Act One include enough scenes that will adequately introduce my main character and his history, motivations, flaws, and desires?
- Why should your reader care about your characters? Have you developed him enough for your reader to feel an adequate level of investment?
- By the second or third scene, does my novel begin to introduce or hint at the latent or overt conflicts that face my main character?
- Is the first third of my novel interesting? Does enough happen?
- By the end of Act One, is my character forced or compelled to act on his yearnings? What is at stake for my character if he doesn't get what he wants?

Act Two

Act Two is the heart of your novel, the meat and bones, the weighty bulk, the middle seas, the sandwich stuffing. You get the point. It's where your character is faced with obstacles, either internal or external, and responds in a way that moves your story forward. The middle part of your novel raises the stakes for your character; your character wants something (an objective), and something is standing in her way (a complication). Remember what fiction writer Anne Lamott once said, "[Y]ou are probably going to have to let bad things happen to some of the characters you love or you won't have much of a story." And she is absolutely right. As much as you love your characters—let's face it, you've spent a lot of time with them!—you cannot let them have exactly what they want the moment they want it. Giving your characters what they want is a surefire way to kill your story. Remember perfect Mary? And her two perfect children? And that perfect house in the suburbs? And her perfect, moneymaking husband? I'm getting sleepy again ... zzzzz ....

You were asked earlier in this assignment to make a list of the ways in which your character's yearnings were thwarted or blocked. Did you find enough obstacles to sustain two-hundred-plus pages? If not, you'll need to adjust your outline so as to raise the stakes for your protagonist. What does your character stand to gain? What does she stand to lose?

At the end of Act Two, the tension, of course, needs to come to a boiling point—or a boiling-over point. Some refer to this as the crisis moment or the make-or-break-moment your character faces. Your character must make a realization, of sorts, and this realization will play out in the climax scene. This scene dramatizes the themes and conflicts that you, the author, have been trying to convey through your written portraits of your character and his world, scene by scene. In some ways, the climax is the most important moment in your novel, for within this scene your protagonist will come face-to-face with a choice that must fundamentally change him. I like to think of the climax as the point of no return. Your character has wandered too deep into the woods to turn around; the only way to escape is the move forward (unless these are the woods from *The Blair Witch Project*, in which case, there is no escape).

Really take some time to examine the second third of your novel, and ask yourself the following questions:

90 DAYS TO YOUR NOVEL

- Have you deepened the conflict for your characters? What obstacles stand between your character and what she wants?
- Where could you stand to add further complications for your protagonist?
- How are my character's motivations, desires, and values causing him to react to events and situations in a way particular to him?
- How is my character changing from Act One? Is he changing or staying the same in the face of changes around him? How is he affected by the events unfolding before him?
- What is the climax of my novel? What is the key moment for my protagonist in his quest for self-understanding?

Act Three

Act Three, as a whole, should do several things at once. First, you'll need to tie up any loose ends for your reader. Even minor plot points will need to be resolved in this section—so, for example, that man lurking in the shadows in a few of your earlier scenes will need to be revealed. Was he a super-creepy stalker of your protagonist Josephine? Her guardian angel? The father she never knew? You'll need to explain the lurker to your readers, lest you risk frustrating them.

What about that kiss Josephine shared with Arnold in chapter four? It seemed like they might have made a connection—a love connection à la Chuck Woolery—but Arnold hasn't been seen in your novel since. (Maybe Josephine was too busy trying to figure out who the man lurking in the shadows was.) In Act Three, even minor characters will have to be brought back onstage to wrap up any unresolved issues. Does Arnold have feelings for Josephine? Does Josephine reciprocate them? Will Arnold be the manifestation, for Josephine, of the man she's been tracking down her entire life? (Her absent father, perhaps? Is he the man who lurks in shadows?)

In addition, you'll need to reveal the consequences, for your character, of the climax scene. Who has been affected by your protagonist's actions and reactions in the "key scene" of your novel?

Let's consider the example of that old sport Jay Gatsby again. The climax of *The Great Gatsby* is the public revelation of Gatsby and Daisy's affair. After this point nothing can ever be quite the same for him. What might naturally happen, then? Well, for one, Tom Buchanan is not going to be happy. No, sir. Daisy is his wife, after all, and even if he did have his own affair with Myrtle, he *owns* Daisy. The fallout of Gatsby's reunion with Daisy manifests itself in several ways, both big and small: Daisy refuses to leave Tom, thus shattering Gatsby's dreams. Daisy rushes off in Gatsby's car, accidentally hitting Myrtle, killing her. Tom pins the blame on Gatsby, and poor Gatsby, well, in the end he was not so great: He was found dead, shot to death by Myrtle's father. All this fallout happened *because* of the climax scene: Gatsby's reunion with his lost love.

Your climax scene is the first domino that causes the chain reaction in your story. What else in your fictional world will be affected by it? You'll need to be sure your reader feels you've fully resolved the story, even if the resolution isn't necessarily a happy one.

At this point, I want you to take a look at the final third of your outline and ask yourself:

- What plot points have you left unresolved thus far?

- Which minor characters deserve a few final pages in Act Three?
- Does your outline, as you've written it, contain enough substance? Does it wrap up the loose ends of your novel?
- Does your outline contain a scene that reveals the consequences for your characters in terms of how they acted and reacted to the climax scene?
- Does your outline contain a scene or scenes that show *how* your protagonist has changed from the start of your novel?
- What kind of ending do you imagine for your novel? Does the protagonist get what he wants in the end? Does the protagonist *not* get what he wants? Is it a combination ending, where the main character gets what he wants (but in the end he realizes that's a bad thing) or doesn't get what he wants (but in the end realizes this is for the best)?

If you are unable to answer any of the above questions, I'd like you to spend some time revising your outline. Remember, outlines are only guides, and you should not consider yours to be a fixed entity. Now that you've thought through and outlined a good chunk of your novel, perhaps it's a better idea for your character *not* to get what she wants in the end. Perhaps Josephine realizes she's madly in love with Arnold, but it's too late: All this time and energy she's spent searching for her father has ruined her. Arnold's lost interest, and Josephine needs to take a good, long look in the mirror and realize the negative impact of her obsession with her father, a man she may never know. Women can be so fickle.

The more time you spend tinkering with your outline now, the more time and freedom you'll have to write in the following weeks. And that's what the real goal is here, right?

WEEK 4, ASSIGNMENT 4:
Researching Your Fictional World

Perhaps you read the title of this assignment and said to yourself: *Research? I'm a fiction writer! I don't need no stinking research!*

The amount of research required for a novel will, of course, depend on multiple factors. Is your novel set in a historical time period? If so, you'll need to do a hefty bit of research on the kinds of style, trends, and current events of that era. Would your characters be more likely to wear bell-bottoms or corsets? Is your novel set in Cincinnati, Ohio? If so, what are the various parts of town? What does the geography look like? Is it flat or hilly there? (Hint: Cincinnati is known as the city of seven hills.) Even if your novel is set in a fictional Midwestern town, you should know the topography of the region in order to sustain the believability of your descriptions. What animals are indigenous to the region? How about plants? If you include a palm tree in a Midwestern setting, you'll likely turn off even those readers who have never driven through the region.

Maybe your character is the wealthiest man in the world and buys only the most exquisite items. What is the most expensive kind of car? Do you know what it looks like? How would the interior leather feel? What is an expensive, high-end brand of suits or shoes or handbags? These might be important details in your novel.

What is the occupation of your character(s)? Are they thieving stockbrokers? Humble Bible salesmen? Pathological speech pathologists? If you don't know much about these occupations, you'll need to at least learn the vocabulary of the trade. Joanna Scott's novel *The Manikin*, for example, is set in the rural home of a prominent taxidermist. How convincing a portrait of a taxidermist could Scott have created if she didn't know anything about taxidermy? Probably not a very realistic one. It should come as no surprise, then, to learn that Scott did extensive research on taxidermy while writing the novel, visiting several taxidermists in person so she could write from the vantage point of experience.

Many authors conduct research prior to writing their novels. The key to writing convincingly on any subject is to know the subject so well that it becomes an inherent, natural part of your storytelling. That is, you must understand the profession of taxidermy so well you begin to reason, act, and, most certainly, write as a taxidermist would.

Spend a minimum of two hours conducting cursory research on the various elements of your story, and take notes. You may use this information—or you may not. Such is the nature of research. Not everything you find will be equally useful. The easiest way to conduct research these days is, of course, the Internet. But be careful—not all sites have credible information. You'll want to check your sources. Does your information come from the American Academy of Taxidermists or some woman named Liz who lives in her grandma's basement? The difference is a big one. Your local librarian might be interested in helping an aspiring novelist with a few research pointers, too, but you'll have to step up and ask.

Another useful way to learn about a particular subject is to do field research. If you're writing a novel about a maniacal serial-killer butcher, for example, visit your local butcher shop and speak with the head meat cutter there. What do butchers' knives look like? How much do they cost? What does a meat locker smell like? Would it be a good place to stash a body? Or maybe you want to talk to the receptionist at a chiropractor's office. (But be sure to use a whisper—doctor's waiting rooms are oddly quiet places, you'll find, if you do your research.)

WHAT A CHARACTER

Nearly one-third of your ninety-day writing challenge is behind you. How do you feel about it? If you're anything like me, it may be difficult to look at the progress you've made when all that work still lies ahead. But you should stop (briefly) to reward yourself for passing this important mile marker. Buy yourself an overpriced coffee, maybe a grande super mocha vanilla soy milk frappaccino with whipped cream and caramel. Or buy yourself a glass of wine or a cold beer, if that suits you better. Maybe a glass of sherry to swill would more aptly match your writer's persona. But you realize that there's no such thing as a writer's persona—only the sweat on a writer's brow.

You've been at work on your novel for nearly a month now, and if you've been diligently following the schedule this book sets, you've most certainly made some major headway. By this point, you have a working outline that has been tested, assessed, and revised for variety, pacing, and an even narrative arc. You now know where you want to begin your novel, and where you want to end it. You know what story you want to tell, and, by Jove, you just want to get started already. And start we will....

If you were expecting to start with your opening scene, don't despair. The work you accomplish in this chapter will likely be revised and incorporated into various subsequent scenes listed on your outline. However, we're not ready yet to dive into that first scene of the novel. We've got one more week of assignments to explore first, and these assignments can really make or break your novel.

Earlier we discussed how characters are the single most important element of your novel, for the decisions you make about who your characters will be affect nearly every other aspect of your novel. Your character's mood impacts the tone of your novel; your character's disposition might affect how he sees and interprets the setting; how your character dresses or where he lives will go a long way toward revealing his interiority; how your character responds to the events unfolding before him will alter the plot of your novel. And so on. Even in plot-driven novels or genre novels, readers want characters they can connect with, people they can empathize with and understand, individuals they feel they know as well as real, flesh-and-blood humans.

This week our assignments will focus on writing scenes that further develop your character. You may use and revise many of these scenes in the following weeks as we approach your novel in a more linear fashion, starting from your first scenes and moving to your last ones. Or you may find that as you develop your characters and move forward with your outlines, your character has developed in a different direction. The goal of the following assignments is not to simply describe your characters' personality traits and attributes, but to reveal them *in scene*. This is where character development gets tricky. Remember that in fiction, like cooking an exquisite meal, you can't separate the discrete elements and hope to come out with a cohesive final product. You must consider all the elements of scene construction in order to make your characters leap off the page. As you know by now, you must appeal to your readers' senses and emotions.

WEEK 5, ASSIGNMENT 1: *You Are How You Look*

I'd like you to return to the assignment you composed for Day 10 for a moment. Print out a copy and find a highlighter or a colored pen. In this particular assignment, you were asked to write a scene that introduces your protagonist and reveals your character's interiority, motivations, and desires. Take a few minutes assessing this scene. Then highlight the places in this scene where you use concrete, tactile description. From each highlighted section, draw a line out to the margin. For each sentence or phrase of physical description, I want you to write a brief sentence assessing what you think this physical feature reveals about your character's personality or disposition. If your character has a furrowed brow and forehead wrinkles that look like they were drawn with a permanent marker, what do you think this reveals? I hope this character isn't a happy-go-lucky hippie who hasn't a care in the world. If your character is a young girl with rose-colored cheeks, what does this say? Is there any way this young lass could have a malevolent interior? Could these rosy cheeks distract you from her squinty, dead-still eyes?

Character appearance, dress, and overall presentation is yet another way that fiction reflects the real world. Just as you'd make character judgments about a woman wearing fire-engine-red lipstick, six-inch stilettos, and a formfitting leopard-skin dress—yes, everyone judges sometimes, even a little bit—so will your readers make judgments about the interiority of your character based on his or her exterior. Our judgments are not always initially correct, mind you, but you'll be left with an indelible first impression. The details you use to describe your character will go a long way toward forming an overall impression.

Now I want you to revise the above scene, paying particular attention to writing with the senses and showing how the exterior reflects the interior. How does your character's overall presentation—body language, dress, physique, speech—tell a story about who that individual really is? Does her interior reflect her exterior? See if you can tuck bits of physical description here and there, throughout the scene. Avoid dumping in too much data at once. Think about how you would personally size someone up upon first meeting. What kinds of things do you notice first? You certainly don't notice every physical feature at once.

Because we're focusing, too, on scene writing, make sure your scene has a clear beginning, middle, and end. What is the conflict of this scene? If you need to, take another look at the chapter on scene structure (see page 36) for guidance.

WEEK 5, ASSIGNMENT 2:
Sharply Particular Characters

In his essay "Not-Knowing," fiction writer Donald Barthelme writes, "The world enters the work as it enters our ordinary lives, not as worldview or system but in sharp particularity." What Barthelme means here is that the world, and the characters in it, must enter your work with a certain amount of specific, concrete detail. And these details should be both *sharp and particular* to the character you are introducing. In other words, no other character's habits, customs, mannerisms, and words could be quite the same. Think about the way Kramer enters Jerry's apartment on *Seinfeld*, for example. He swings open the door and spastically shimmy-slides into the room. Kramer embodies exactly the kind of sharp particularity Barthelme means. Nobody enters a room quite like Kramer, and his odd entrances are emblematic of the crazed and quirky nature of the character himself. Your details should be such that the world and the character in your novel become immediately realized.

The first time you introduce characters in your novel, you should be cognizant of giving them immediate distinguishing features (in terms of their physical appearance, mannerisms, or behaviors) that will help lodge them in the minds of your readers. If your novel has quite a few characters, you should pay close attention to establishing personalities and traits that are distinct enough from one another. If three of your female characters are blonde, how will your reader distinguish one from the other? Does one tilt her head to the side so frequently that she's developed a protruding neck muscle? Does another have a voice so low you'd think it was your grandfather's? Does the third one really have dark roots and black eyebrows—so you just know she's not a natural blonde, that liar, you just know it.

But keep in mind, you don't want to simply provide paragraph after paragraph of physical descriptions. This would be tedious, and, furthermore, it isn't really how anyone sizes up another individual upon first meeting. Think about it: Suppose you are meeting Nicola, the den mother of your son's Boy Scout troop, to pick up some merit badges. At first, you might notice the size of the woman—she's at least 6'3"! But then you have a bit of conversation, perhaps. She hands you those badges, and you accept the bundle. That's when you notice her particularly large and hairy hand, with pink acrylic nails filed to a point. You exchange a few words, and you say something to make her smile. This is when you notice her teeth—jagged like a cat's. The point is that your descriptions of characters should come it bits and pieces throughout the scene—not just in one large data dump. Balance, balance, balance. When you write in scene, as you'll be doing from here on out, you'll need to pay particular attention to balancing the various elements of narrative.

Now I want you to write a long scene from your outline in which a new character is introduced for the first time. The character you choose can be either your main protagonist or another one of your main players. How can you bring this character quickly into focus? In this scene pay attention to coming up with sharp, original details particular to your character. What about your character will immediately reveal his nature? Would he enter the room with a BAM! or more meekly poke his head in the door, looking around before he whispers in a shaky voice, "Hello?" Because this is a scene, you'll want to pay attention to all the elements of scene. How does your character speak? To whom is she speaking? What does the setting look like? What will the conflict be in this scene? Perhaps the most difficult aspect of writing is keeping all these details in your mind at once. If it helps, place a small sticky note on your desk that reads *The Scene is a Balancing Act*.

WEEK 5, ASSIGNMENT 3: *Conducting Background Checks*
Take another look at your outline and tally the number of characters who populate your novelistic world. Be sure to count both the minor and major players. How many do

you see? Is the cast large enough to hold the weight of two-hundred-plus pages? If you haven't done so already, I want you to double-check to make sure you've filled out a character bio sheet for each of these individuals (See pages 61 and 107 for the bio sheets for major and minor characters).

Like humans, fictional characters are the sum of their experiences. And it's vital that you know your character's histories, occupations, desires, and motivations before you're too far into the heart of your novel. Remember, once you begin writing your novel, you don't want to have to stop to rework your characters; they should be fundamentally realized, in your mind, from the start. This will allow you the freedom to write without constraints, and you'll be able to focus more clearly on developing your characters and your story instead of dealing with the logistics.

Remember, how a character acts or reacts to a given situation will probably result from her history. Think about our old friend Jay Gatsby again. What was his history, and how did it affect his present actions within F. Scott Fitzgerald's novel? The novel reveals that he was born Jimmy Gatz, a poor boy from Minnesota. He tried to remake himself, met Daisy, and fell in love with her, but he lost her when he went away to war and she married Tom Buchanan. Poor sport. The reader knows, too, that Gatsby involved himself in some shady business, probably even criminal activity. How, then, would these details of Gatsby's history affect his forward-going actions? Would this make it more likely or less likely that he'd do whatever he could to impress the woman he loved? More likely. Would he throw over-the-top, lavish parties to try to impress her? Yes. Would he buy books but never open them just to populate his house with extravagant, copious *things*? Uh-huh. Would his history as Mr. Nobody from Nowhere drive him to desperate, obsessive measures to get what he wanted from life? Certainly.

A good way to include small amounts of history is by using the technique of flashback. When you use flashback, as you recall from your lesson in Day 17, you are literally showing the reader glimpses of scenes, events, moments that happened *prior* to the present time of your novel. So, for instance, if your novel begins when your protagonist is thirty-seven years old, you may choose to flashback to her wedding day, when she was thirty, to the birth of her first child, when she was thirty-three, and to her subsequent divorce from her no-good, two-timing husband when she was thirty-five.

Take a look at this example, again from *The Hours* by Michael Cunningham. In this passage, one of the three central protagonists, a dissatisfied housewife named Laura Brown, is meditating upon how she met and married her husband:

> She inhales deeply. It is so beautiful; it is so much more than ... well, than almost anything, really. In another world, she might have spent her whole life reading. But this is the new world, the rescued world—there's not much room for idleness. So much has been risked and lost; so many have died. Less than five years ago Dan himself was believed to have died, at Anzio, and when he was revealed two days later to be alive after all (he and some poor boy from Arcadia had had the same name) it seemed he had been resurrected. He seemed to have returned, still sweet-tempered, still smelling like himself, from the realm of the dead ... and when he came back to California he was received as something more than an ordinary hero. He could (in the words of his own alarmed mother) have had anyone, any pageant winner, any vivacious and compliant girl, but through some obscure and possibly perverse genius had kissed, courted, and proposed to his best

friend's older sister, the bookworm, the foreign-looking one with the dark, close-set eyes and the Roman nose, who had never been sought after or cherished; who had always been left alone, to read. What could she say but yes? How could she deny a handsome, good-hearted boy, practically a member of the family, who had come back from the dead?

So now she is Laura Brown. Laura Zielski, the solitary girl, the incessant reader, is gone, and in her place is Laura Brown.

At the start of this passage, Laura Brown is in the present moment of the novel, thinking in a seemingly innocuous way about her surroundings, the book she's reading, and her current life. Then, seamlessly, she flashes back in time and reflects on her husband and the reasons she married him in the first place. He was a soldier returning from war, and she was a woman who was rarely desired. Cunningham uses a moment of flashback here to explain some of the reason's for Laura's discontent and to rationalize—for both the character of Laura and for the reader—the reasons she decided to marry in the first place. This reasoning will go a long way toward providing a glimpse into Laura's motivations—and her actions later in the novel. No spoilers here, but the book is a fine example of how to interweave the past, the present, and the future.

However, remember the rules that govern flashbacks: You should never flashback for such a long period of time that your reader finds himself forgetting what the present story, or the "real" story, of the novel is. That is, if you have a tendency to flashback too often, perhaps you've not started your novel in the right place. Do you have a recurring urge to return to your character's time working in the coal mines before he became institutionalized? Perhaps you should instead start your novel deep in the mining shafts, with only a single light from your character's helmet to guide the reader. Flashing back too often can be very distracting to the forward plot of your novel; your writer will grow dizzy from moving backward and forward in time so often. Be aware of this as you write. Instead you should try to stash bits of flashback in a couple of sharp, revealing sentences or paragraphs "hidden" within your scene.

Write a long scene from your outline that narrates the present moments of your novel while also showing your character wanting something out of reach. Be sure to include at least two other characters in this scene, and pay attention to revealing the nuances of all characters involved. What are their appearances, histories, and motivations? How has the past of the character affected the present and the choices he makes?

WEEK 5, ASSIGNMENT 4: *Becoming a Mind Reader*

Your previous assignments for this week have all focused on character development through physical, sensory details or through exploring your character's backstory. For this assignment, however, I want you to try your best to get inside your main character's mind. Everybody thinks, rationalizes, and reasons differently, and how your main or POV character thinks and reasons will profoundly influence the voice of your work. A novel narrated by a corrupt cop will sound different—tonally, rhythmically, and content-wise—than a novel narrated by a kindly alpaca farmer. Each of these individuals will filter the world through different lenses, and each will have a particular manner of describing scenes to the reader.

You practiced drawing out the voice of your POV character in your exercise for Day 9. Take out or print out this scene in which you were asked to write, and reread it. What can you tell about the character you portrayed in this scene simply through *how* this scene is narrated? Think about its style, rhythm, sentence structure, and diction. Take a few minutes and read the first page or two out loud. What are you able to tell about the personality of the POV character? Are your sentences long or short? Is your vocabulary elevated or dumbed down? Take out a highlighter and spend a few moments locating any word, sentence, or phrasing that seems particularly representative of the character who is narrating this scene.

Many novels hinge on both what a character is thinking and *how* this character thinks. Although a certain amount of plotted action is crucial to any novel, learning exactly how your main character thinks will help you best narrate these scenes of actions.

I want you to try your best to get inside your narrator's head. Take on your character's persona. Dress like them as you write, if you want to take it that far. You are now Peggy, a server at Big Ben's Food Mart in London, or Randolph, a used-car salesman with aspirations toward becoming a Broadway tap-dancing star. For this exercise, you are not you. Instead you are your main character. What's it like to be in this body? What does it feel like? Are you more or less confident than you are now? Are you more or less self-conscious? What kinds of things do you notice or pay attention to that you might have missed if you were you?

Select a scene from the first part of your outline and write a long scene from this distinctive perspective. What does your character see? And what does he think about the scene that unfolds before him? Try not to hold back at this point—remember, you'll be editing and reworking the scenes from this week to use later in your novel. If your character wants to pass gas, let him. Nobody's listening ... yet. The goal is to as closely approximate your character's thinking, feeling, and sensing as possible. You want your reader to *hear* your protagonist's voice.

WEEK 5, ASSIGNMENT 5: *Eyeballing It*

The final assignment for this week is very closely related to character development and voice—the elements of fiction you've been working on in the past four assignments. As you know from the last exercise, who you select to tell your story—or the perspective the reader is given in the story—will greatly affect how your story gets told. Think about it: Let's say a huge explosion goes off and only four bystanders are there to witness it. Here's how they may respond:

> **Person one:** Oh, my gravy!
>
> **Person two:** Holy S*@$! Run for it!
>
> **Person three:** Call 9-1-1! Quick! Somebody call 9-1-1!!! I'll see if anyone is hurt.
>
> **Person four:** I did *not* have anything to do with the explosion. I wasn't even near it.
>
> **Person five:** (Silently blinks.)

Person two wants to run away from the problem, while person three wants to run toward it to see if others need help. Person one, from the diction, sounds a little bit like a country kitty. Maybe she's seen fires like this before when she's burned brush piles. Person four immediately declares his innocence. Why might that be? Does he have a criminal record? Person five is silent, of course. And silence sometimes speaks louder than words.

Each of these five individuals, depending on his personality traits, backgrounds, and levels of fear, will report the explosion in a different way, using different details.

Select a scene from early in your outline that contains some action and interaction between multiple characters. Now write two short scenes. The first scene should be narrated from your main character's POV. The second scene should be this same scene narrated from another character's POV. Remember to pay close attention to how the POV character is interpreting the unfolding events.

Now try a similar thing with your very first scene. Write one short scene in the first person and one in the third person. When you are finished with all four short scenes, reread and analyze them. Ask yourself which perspective is the most interesting. Have you selected the appropriate POV character to narrate your novel?

WHERE IT ALL BEGINS
The First Scene(s)

For the next several weeks, we'll be kicking it into high gear. Be sure to eat your protein and get enough sleep. Hydrate. You'll need all the energy you can find to barrel through these coming assignments, and trust me, there will be days when you'd rather stay in bed and sleep. There will be days when you wish you hadn't signed that contract with yourself to write this #$!* novel. But many days will also find you wholly energized by the process. You may even find yourself writing for longer periods of time than the mandated two to three hours as you lose yourself inside your fictional world. The most important part is to try to enjoy yourself, and this enjoyment will come across in your prose. Nothing is worse than a writer who takes himself too seriously.

In the previous lessons, we focused on some discrete components of your novel: developing characters, selecting the appropriate POV and narration technique, and charting the arc of your novel. Now I want to go back to the start. Literally. I want you to begin working on the first scene of your novel. Finally!

Cue the music: Hallelujah! Hallelujah! Hallelujah, Hallelujah! Hall-eee-luuu-jah!

In the next several weeks, we'll be examining your novel in a more linear fashion, from the gripping first pages to stake-raising middle scenes, and, finally, to the compelling culminating scenes. We still have a lot of work ahead of us, but hopefully by now, with the necessary tools in place, you'll be ready to write without restraint or interruption. You only have fifty-four days to go! Hop to it. Chop-chop.

The first few paragraphs of your novel will help a reader determine whether or not she wants to buy the book, and the first scene or chapter will determine if your reader will continue your book. As such, it's absolutely essential to begin your novel in the right place, in the right moment, with the right character, and in the right manner. Remember, where you begin your novel shouldn't be left to random chance. Think through the decision, and ask yourself why you think the beginning you've selected is the right one.

In the previous lesson, we talked a bit about the general function of Act One of your novel. In this portion of your novel, you'll introduce your characters, their histories, and the underlying conflicts. Act One is the buildup to the novel's core—and as you all know, the better the buildup, the bigger the payout. But you'll also want to make the reader feel immersed immediately in your novelistic world. Why should they continue their stay in *your* fictional land, after all, if they have so many other options? Readers won't do you any favors, so it's best to immediately drop any preconceived notions of your fiction's greatness. You've got to earn your readers, one page at a time.

WEEK 6, ASSIGNMENT 1: *The First Lines*

Think of the first lines of your novel as the moment you open the door to meet your blind date—what's your first impression? Is he wearing a mock turtleneck sporting a beer logo? Does his heavy usage of hair gel cast reflections on the wall? Or is his broad smile inviting, framed by pillowy lips that could only be that of a trumpet player? Your novel's first impression on the reader, those first few sharp lines, will begin to put your fictional world into a sharp and particular perspective. The first lines also serve as literary bait, enticing your reader to continue on with the next few lines, then the next few lines, until, suddenly, they are knee-deep in your story, committed to reading the rest. The goal of any author, as we've discussed, is always to keep the reader reading, the pages turning. As an author, you should want your novels to get banged up and dog-eared by your reader, a sign that they've been read with eager intent.

Of course, there are many ways to begin a scene, but for the very first scene of your novel, it's a good idea to provide a hook of some sort for your reader. In a previous section, I described the hook as you probably learned it in a college or high school writing class: It's an attention-grabbing set of lines that immediately captures the minds of your readers, lines that compel them to read further. Local news broadcasts often provide hooks, sometimes called teasers, to encourage their viewers to tune in for the next broadcast. "Gangs of violent billy goats roaming the streets of our city. When will their bleating get to your neighborhood, and how will this affect … *your children*? Details at eleven." You find yourself tuning in for the evening broadcast—what neighborhood are these goat gangs menacing now? Where might they roam next? And just how loud is that bleating? You've been hooked. (Or hoodwinked.)

A good first line is an invitation to your readers to join these particular characters inside your novelistic world.

Strong scene openings immediately engage readers through physical descriptions and emotional connections. And, of course, through revelation of conflict. (Keep in mind Kurt Vonnegut who once said: "Every character should want something, even if it is only a glass of water.)

I'd like for you to take out your completed assignment for Day 14. In this assignment, you were asked to write twenty first lines for your novel that introduced your character and the conflict immediately. On a separate piece of paper, for a few minutes, I want you to analyze the strength of each sentence. For each line, I want you to ask yourself, *Is my world/character entering the novel in sharp particularity? Are the details concrete? Is this first line memorable? How could I make this sentence stronger?*

Consider, for a moment, the first lines of Alice Sebold's popular novel *The Lovely Bones*:

"My name was Salmon, like the fish; first name, Susie. I was fourteen when I was murdered on December 6, 1973."

The first lines of this novel instantly grab the attention of the audience. First, we get a bit of insight into Susie: She's young and naive enough to still introduce herself as "Salmon, like the fish." This is a detail particular to Susie's personality, and the line immediately lends to the book's childlike narrative quality. The second sentence thrusts the reader directly into the conflict. Our young protagonist was murdered—and thus we can conclude that she's narrating this novel from the great beyond. This particular hook hooked millions of readers and earned Sebold a movie contract.

Now consider this first line from Ralph Ellison's classic, *The Invisible Man*: "I am an invisible man." Such a spare line as this one would prompt the reader to immediately question, *Why are you invisible? Are you a ghost? Will this be a supernatural story? Are you simply metaphorically invisible?* Good hooks plant questions in the readers' minds, questions they must seek through further reading.

Finally, take a look at these first lines from Jeffrey Eugenides's 1993 novel *The Virgin Suicides:*

> On the morning the last Lisbon daughter took her turn at suicide—it was Mary this time, and sleeping pills, like Therese—the two paramedics arrived at the house knowing exactly where the knife drawer was, and the gas oven, and the beam in the basement from which it was possible to tie a rope. They got out of the EMS truck, as usual moving much too slowly in our opinion, and the fat one said under his breath, "This ain't TV, folks, this is how fast we go." He was carrying the heavy respirator and cardiac unit past the bushes that had grown monstrous and over the erupting lawn, tame and immaculate thirteen months earlier when the trouble began.

What a dose of information the reader receives in these first few lines! Eugenides provides ample description of setting (paramedics are arriving at the Lisbon house, and they've been there before), character introductions (Therese and Mary Lisbon), POV indicators ("our opinion" reveals a collective narrator), and conflict (the Lisbon sisters have all committed suicide, and the root of it all began thirteen months ago). This brilliant opening piques the interest of even the most casual reader, and I'd be willing to bet that anyone who read those first few lines will be intrigued to read on further. It should come as no surprise, then, that this novel, like *The Lovely Bones*, was also a national bestseller that went on to become a major motion picture.

Go back to your list of twenty opening lines and select one. If you must, revise this line to add any necessary sharp and particular detail, and now write a second line. Have you revealed a conflict yet? Hinted at it? Why did you start at this moment instead of another? What is the significance of this particular moment in relation to the rest of your novel? Spend some time focusing on the first lines of your novel, playing around with the twenty initial lines you originally penned. Which one will hook the reader faster? Which is most interesting? While you don't want to get stuck on the first few lines of this novel, you also don't want to undervalue the importance of these sentences.

WEEK 6, ASSIGNMENT 2: *Scene One, Take One*

In the very first pages, like in your first few lines, you'll need to introduce your reader to your character(s) in such a way that your reader feels immediately invested. You want your readers to feel like they *already* know your characters. Your characters should enter a world with such a burst of energy and a familiarity, your readers should feel that if they tune out or stop reading for even a moment they'll actually miss something. (Have you ever stepped out to get popcorn at the start of a movie? If so, you know the feeling.)

Let's take a moment to consider, again, the opening of *The Lovely Bones*. This time I'll provide a few paragraphs:

> My name was Salmon, like the fish; first name, Susie. I was fourteen when I was murdered on December 6, 1973. In newspaper photos of missing girls from the seventies, most looked like me: white girls with mousy brown hair. This was before kids of all races and genders started appearing on milk cartons or in the daily mail. It was still back when people believed things like that didn't happen.

In my junior high yearbook I had a quote from a Spanish poet my sister had turned me on to, Juan Ramon Jimenez. It went like this: "If they give you ruled paper, write the other way." I chose it both because it expressed my contempt for my structured surroundings a la the classroom and because, not being some dopey quote from a rock group, I thought it marked me as literary....

I wasn't killed by Mr. Botte, by the way. Don't think every person you're going to meet in here is a suspect. That's the problem. You never know....My murderer was a man from our neighborhood.

Before you read on, I want you to ask yourself the following questions and take the time to answer them, if only in your head:

- What did you learn about the character so far?
- What do you know about the plot so far?
- What are some of the conflicts or complications?
- Did you feel drawn into the story? Why?

We learn quite a bit about the novel and about Susie, the novel's protagonist, in this paragraph. We learn immediately that she's been murdered. By a neighbor. (The fact that she names her murderer tells us this won't be whodunit novel.) We know she has a sister who turned her on to a Spanish poet (and this detail tells us something about the sister, too). We also know quite a bit about her history: Susie was in every way a typical teenager at the time of her death. She was concerned with what others thought of her, with "seeming literary," and she manifests the typical contempt for the structure of school of an average teenager. But Susie is no average teenager. She's dead, and she's narrating from beyond the grave. Those are significant and compelling facts, don't you think?

A general rule to keep in mind is this: The first scene belongs to your protagonist, and as such, it's vital to introduce your protagonist as early as possible—in the first line, if you can. While long descriptions of setting or character, or philosophical ruminations, do have a place in your novel, waiting too long to introduce your protagonist or the conflict can be a novel-killing decision. In the first scene, you should be paying more attention to quick pacing than to lengthy paragraphs of exposition. You want your reader to keep turning the pages—to feel like she is already making progress in the novel. As such, you should try to reveal some sort of conflict or tension within the first pages. Even in the first lines cited above from the works of Sebold, Ellison, and Eugenides, you are able to discern a conflict within the first few words.

In your first scene, consider these tips:

- Scene opening: Hook your reader with a compelling first line—or set of lines—that hints at a conflict.

- Be sure to explain the significance of the novel's starting point. (In *The Lovely Bones*, for example, the significance of the starting is an event: the murder of Susie Salmon.)

- Provide insight to your character through dialogue, bits of physical description, and indirect thought. By the end of the first scene, we should know a significant amount of your character's history.

- Readers relate to your world through physical, tactile description. Be sure to describe the setting and what your character sees, feels, smells, hears, etc.

- Pay attention to pacing. In the first few pages *especially*, avoid any overly lengthy descriptions of setting or interior thoughts. Orient your reader with concrete details first!

- By the middle of the first scene, your character should be faced with a conflict. What is at stake for your character in this scene? You should turn your readers' expectations upside down by putting your character in an unusual or unexpected situation. If your protagonist is a priest, what would happen if he ended up at a disco, for instance? If your character is claustrophobic, what would happen if she were to be trapped in a meat locker? How would this be made worse if your character were a claustrophobic vegetarian trapped in that meat locker?

- Scene ending: Leave your first scene with an unresolved situation, so your reader will remain curious enough to read the next scene. While all novels don't have that can't-put-down quality, it never hurts to aim for it in a first draft.

This assignment asks you to write your first scene, paying attention to the techniques discussed above. If you've already written your first scene during the assignment for Day 14, revise this scene with an eye toward building conflict and developing character. Spend a good deal of time on this assignment. These first pages will be the most important ones for earning a readership.

WEEK 6, ASSIGNMENT 3: *In the Middle of the Beginning*
If you're reading this, and if you're following these assignments completely and in order (as you should be because

you signed a contract with yourself) you've already written the first scene of your novel. And if you've written the first scene of your novel, you know how difficult wrestling a scene into shape can be. It's all about balance, you know, including enough of each discrete component of fiction to paint a world in full color. You can't just tell your reader about your protagonists, setting, and conflicts—you must let your reader experience it on her own. It's pretty tricky, but, remember, nobody said you'd get it perfect on your first try.

Take another look for a moment at your outline. As you know from two weeks ago when we assessed your outline and your novel's narrative arc, something must happen by the end of the first act of your novel. This something, either internal or external, will compel or otherwise force your protagonist to action within the confines of your novel. What is this major plot point? In *Romeo and Juliet*, for example, the end of Act One finds Juliet in love. "My only love sprung from my only hate!" she squeals as she learns from her nurse that the man she's fallen in love with (and so quickly, too) is the son of her family's sworn enemy. Oh, no! This first major plot point is what precipitates the other actions of the play. But, remember, *Romeo and Juliet* is a five-act play. What happens roughly one-third of the way through this dramatic tragedy? The two marry, of course. And it is this plotted point—this marital act—that becomes the undoing for each, leading to the climax and the unfortunate double suicide of these two young lovers.

What is the first major plot point that occurs in the first act of your novel? How many scenes away from the first scene is it? The first major plot point should fall somewhere near the end of the first act of your novel so that enough time is devoted to developing the characters and the situation. You'll need to keep this first plot point in the back of your mind as you narrate the scenes leading up to this moment.

The goal for this assignment is to write all of the scenes that occur between the first scene and the last scene of the first act of your novel. This may be one long scene, or it may be six shorter ones, depending on the outline you've created. As you write, keep in mind: What kind of information will your reader want or need to know? Where can you develop your character, providing enough flaws to make him sympathetic to your reader? How can you hint at, if not directly reveal, the conflict that your character will face?

Try to write these scenes in as linear a fashion as possible. And even though you should provide a sense of your character's history and past experiences, you should also aim to stay in the present of your novel as much as possible. Remember, flashing back and forth in time too frequently can confuse your reader.

Remember, too, that you need a balance in terms of scene variety. Be sure to include at least one internal scene and one external scene in Act One.

Obviously, if your first act contains several scenes between the first scene and the last scene, you'll have a lot of work to do. But one trick of writing a draft of a novel in ninety days is to balance your time and to recognize that even once you've written your draft, you'll need to go back and revise. While you should give equal weight and time to all assignments, be sure you divvy up your writing days this week to provide enough time for you to complete all of your assignments.

WEEK 6, ASSIGNMENT 4:
The End of the Beginning—or the Start of the End

It's amazing how much writing you can get done if you really set your mind to it. The final assignment for this week is going to focus on the final scene of Act One of your novel. If it's useful to you, think of the final scene of Act One as a mini climax. Your character is faced with a decision, an event, or a circumstance that will naturally lead to the rest of your novel. Perhaps this first plot point is an inheritance, a death, or a journey somewhere they've never been. The possibilities are wide open.

Let's think about the first major plot point in our old faithful example of *The Great Gatsby*. Roughly one-third of the way through the novel we learn that Jay Gatsby, up until this point only revealed thirdhand through the narrator, Nick Carraway, was once in love with Daisy and has moved to West Egg to be near to her. Gatsby has asked Nick to invite his cousin Daisy over for afternoon tea, where Gatsby will unexpectedly show up, surprising Daisy. Nick agrees, Daisy and Gatsby meet, and their affair begins from there. This first plot point sets up the rest of the novel: Daisy and Gatsby's reunion, the revelation of their affair, the death of poor Myrtle, and the murder of Gatsby. None of these events would have been possible without this first major plot point, the reuniting of these two former flames. At this point, Gatsby no longer simply gazes at the green light at the end of Daisy's dock; Daisy's radiant presence has enflamed his old longing.

By the final scene of Act One, you should introduce your reader to the first significant plot point of the novel. What is at stake for your character in this moment? How will his response to this first plot point initiate the events in the next third of your novel?

Fitzgerald ends his first act with a provocative line, indicating the possibilities of Daisy and Gatsby's reunion. Nick says, "Then I went out of the room and down the marble steps into the rain, leaving them there together." The reader might ask, what will they do when they are *alone together*? Read on, good friends, Fitzgerald beckons with this cliffhanger of an ending. Read on.

As you are writing this final scene of Act One, pay particular attention to narrating with all of the senses. Include some dialogue, and be sure to highlight the differences and similarities between what is being outwardly said, what the body language indicates, and what is being inwardly thought by your character.

When you are finished with this final assignment for this week, count your pages, marvel at how much more liberating writing is when you are working with an outline, and celebrate the fact that you are nearly (though not quite) halfway through this ninety-day writing challenge.

WELCOME TO THE MIDDLE

What do the middle of a custard donut and the middle of a novel have in common? Both contain the best part, of course. As you know by now, the middle of your novel—Act Two—is what your novel is really about. When you tell someone what a book or a movie is "about," you usually summarize for her the middle of the novel. For instance, *The Count of Monte Cristo* is about a man, falsely imprisoned for years, who exacts revenge on all those who have wronged him. *The Great Gatsby* is about a man who, obsessed with his former lover, buys a house in her wealthy neighborhood to win her back. *Madame Bovary* is about a woman who has several torrid affairs in an attempt to escape the sheer banality of her life. *Beloved* is about a former slave woman who is haunted by the daughter she killed in order to spare her from slavery. All of these brief recaps essentially summarize Act Two of their respective novels.

Middles are the most important part of your novel and are quite tricky to write. If your reader loses attention or feels the novel is crawling along at a snail's pace or doesn't connect with the protagonist, chances are the problem is located somewhere in the muddled middle. It's particularly important to vary your scene type, pay attention to pacing, and keep an eye toward evolving your characters. Readers want to feel a sense of progression throughout a novel—a sense that things are moving forward.

In some ways, though, the middle is the best, most thought-provoking part to write. Act Two is where you really get the opportunity to explore your characters and their interactions, and your plot and its consequences. And in a novel, you've got plenty of wiggle room to mediate on, say, the history and uses of a pickax or the science behind a flushing toilet. Go ahead and have fun—so long as you stay in character. *Moby-Dick* had an entire chapter about whale facts, for example. People can skip it, but it's the prerogative of the middle to open up a bit. Unlike in a short story, a novel provides more space for a modicum of diversion. (Though you want to be careful not to divert your reader too far from the core of your story, lest you risk losing their interest in it entirely. A subject that you find interesting, such as aquatic flora and fauna, might not be that interesting to someone else.)

The middle of your novel, in fact, is so important that we'll be spending the next three consecutive weeks working on it. Act Two roughly extends from the first major plot point that ended Act One on through to your climax, or the key moment for your character in relation to the story. During this week, we may be writing scenes from our outline a bit out of order, in terms of linearity, but we'll be focusing on drawing out your character through internal scenes. Next week we'll focus on your action scenes, and, finally, the following week, we'll be paying close attention to your novel's climax.

WEEK 7, ASSIGNMENT 1: *Attention: Minors Served Here*

We've already spent a bit of time thinking about scene types and discussing the importance of balancing both internal and external scenes. This week, however, I want to focus a bit more on some of the "internal" scenes in Act Two of your novel. As you know, internal scenes are scenes that work to reveal the inner workings of your character's mind, motivations, or emotions. Often, in internal scenes, your character finds herself alone *or* with a minor character who is used to draw out some sort of personality attribute of your protagonist. Think for a moment, again, of Pammy, a (very) minor character in *The Great Gatsby*. As you remember, Pammy, the daughter of Daisy and Tom Buchanan, is brought into the novel not for the sake of fully revealing her character, but in order to reveal something about Daisy Buchanan. When we see how Daisy treats Pammy—like a possession, modeling her for the dinner guests before shoving her off on the nurse, who carries her away—we understand Daisy's underlying personality issues (or disorders).

Peruse your outline and find a scene where your POV character interacts with a minor character. If you have no scene that involves a minor character—or if you find several scenes in your outline where your protagonist is primarily alone—consider fashioning a minor character to both populate your novelistic world and to uncover a personality trait of your character that may not be uncovered if she were simply alone, gazing at the grand vista from a hilltop. Because think about it: How often do you find yourself completely alone, without interruption, be it the postman, a passing car, or a fellow jogger? (Remember, too, how boring empty landscapes can be.)

Like Pammy in *The Great Gatsby*, not all characters introduced in a novel are self-sufficient. In fact, many characters are flat and unchanging, used only at the service of your lead. Or, like Slugworth in *Charlie and the Chocolate Factory*, some minor characters will fit into the plot later in the novel. If you recall, Slugworth appeared minimally in the first half of the story, tempting the golden-ticket winners to steal an everlasting gobstopper from poor Willy Wonka. However, later in the story, we learn that Slugworth worked for Mr. Wonka as a spy who tested the essential "goodness" of all those sweet-toothed kids. Slugworth was a minor character who served the major ones and became integral to the plot, too, even though his stage time was miniscule.

Your first assignment is to write a long scene paying particular attention to what the interaction between your two characters, one major, one minor, brings to light in your story. Does your character treat the minor character well? Does she barely notice him? Does she cuss at him like a drunken sailor? Does she inwardly think racist or sexist things about him? How do they converse? What is their body language like? Remember, you should always aim to write with the senses. Refer to your character bios as you write in order to make sure you understand the motivations and complexities of each character. And make sure, too, that this scene has a beginning, a middle, and an end. (I'll never tire of reminding you.)

WEEK 7, ASSIGNMENT 2: *Set the Mood Lighting*

Way back on Day 5, you were asked to practice the ways in which setting could be used to reveal character. I'd like you to take out your work from this day and skim it. As you come across any descriptions of physical detail that describes the setting *and* also depicts some aspect of your character, circle it. Hopefully this will remind you of what setting can do—what setting *should do* in a novel.

Setting is not an arbitrary aspect of your novel. You can't simply close your eyes, spin your globe, and decide to set your novel in (spinning my globe now ...) Djibouti near the Gulf of Aden. Heck, you've never even *heard* of Djibouti before, so you don't know what a Djiboutian would look or act like. Instead be intentional in your choice of setting and use it as a tool to help render character, mood, or tone.

I'm going to go out on a limb here and say something that not many fiction writers are supposed to say, and that is, quite bluntly, that long descriptions of setting are boring, even when written by the best of writers. There, I said it. I've been *dying* to get that off my chest for years. What a relief. Yeah, yeah, I'm sure the vista from the hill overlooking the city is stunning—in real life. The hours you spent by the lake, just looking up at that beautiful starry sky, were amazing and vast and profound. All those two-hundred photos you e-mailed me from your hike at Clingmans Dome in the Smokies were (yawn) really great, and I swear I looked at them all in detail. But I don't want to read about an empty landscape with no characters involved. How did the setting make you feel? I want to know. What does it say about you when you remark that you think a plastic grocery bag, swirling slowly in the air in an empty parking lot, is (to borrow from *American Beauty*) the most beautiful thing you've ever seen? In a recent course I taught, the view from the classroom window featured a plastic bag stuck in a tree—a bag that remained there the remainder of the term, irritating me every time I looked at it. Why didn't the maintenance crew every pluck it out? I wanted to know. *These* are the details that will make your setting interesting. And these are the things that will help your setting become an integral part of your novel and not simply a pretty backdrop. Pretty, on its own, is boring. I'd rather save pretty, empty, sweeping views for my hiking, not my reading, thank you very much.

Consider this moment from late in Willa Cather's nostalgic novel *My Ántonia*. In this moment, the novel's protagonist, Jim Burden, has just revisited his beloved (now married, wearied, worn) childhood friend Ántonia after years spent apart. Jim has just confessed to Ántonia that he thinks of her "more than anyone else in the world." Jim longs for a connection to his past on the Nebraska plain. Jim narrates:

> As we walked homeward across the fields, the sun dropped and lay like a great golden globe in the low west. While it hung there, the moon rose in the east, as big as a cart-wheel, pale silver and streaked with rose colour, thin as a bubble or a ghost-moon. For five, perhaps ten minutes, the two luminaries confronted each other across the level land, resting on opposite edges of the work.
>
> In that singular light every little tree and shock of wheat, every sunflower stalk and clump of snow-on-the-mountain, drew itself up high and pointed; the very clods and furrows in the fields seemed to stand up sharply. I felt the odd pull of the earth, the solemn magic that comes out of those fields at nightfall. I wished I could be a little boy again, and that my way could end here.

This setting description parallels Jim's mind-set at this singular moment after revisiting his childhood flame.

He's romanticized his notions of Nebraska, just as he's romanticized Ántonia herself, and his longing for the land and his wistful description of it parallel his interiority. Job well done, Ms. Cather. Not only is the description of the setting specific—a moon as big as a cartwheel is quite precise—but the setting also accomplishes something much more important within the context of the novel: character development.

Take a look at your outline and find an internal scene, perhaps one where your character is alone, or nearly alone. Write this scene using, in part, setting as a primary method for revealing your character's interiority or emotions. You may wish to use the setting, like Cather did above, to mirror the inner workings of your character. Does the sunny day reflect the disposition of your character? Does your character choose to see the positive aspects of the setting: green grass, blooming flowers, chirping birds? Or does he instead only notice the negatives: dirty cobwebs, wet wadded-up newspapers, and dog droppings your snooty neighbor left as a gift in the yard?

WEEK 7, ASSIGNMENT 3: *I Second That Emotion*

Let me back up and say something quite important: Internal and external scenes are not totally rigid distinctions. In fact, they are really fluid categories. For instance, you can use setting to parallel the interiority of your character *in the middle of* a bit of dialogue, which is more external. However, to clarify, if the goal of a scene is to reveal some internal or emotional aspect of your character, that scene is a primarily internal one. If the goal of your scene is to forward the plot or action, that scene is primarily external. Seems pretty simple, right?

This is important to keep in mind as you think about scenes that involve a decent amount of emotional intensity. If you want your novel to have heart—and if you want your reader to connect with your characters—you are going to have to inject an emotional core into your novel. Have you ever read a novel that you, plain and simple, just didn't care about? Perhaps you just didn't care if the big, brawny, muscle-bound man won the petite, green-eyed beauty in the end. The problem for you was that you simply didn't connect with them. Oscar Wilde once said, "A little sincerity is a dangerous thing, and a great deal of it is absolutely fatal." This is an excellent rule of thumb for using emotion in your novel. Too little, and you risk ostracizing your reader. Too much, and you risk your reader getting eye strain from rolling her eyes so much (right before putting down the book, that is). However, in order for your readers to relate to your characters—to care about your characters—the emotions of your characters must be apparent.

When I use the term *emotion* I don't mean the simple-level, touchy-feely kind of emotions you initially connote from the word. Emotions like love, hate, jealousy, fear— these are the basic emotions that form the human experience, yes. But emotions can also be thought of as values. For example, how we feel at a given time, e.g. delighted at seeing someone famous fail as opposed to being sympathetic to them, might signal our own values. How can you connect the values and belief systems of your characters to those of your readers and vice versa? Perhaps your reader has never had to fight tooth and nail for the woman he loves—but he can certainly empathize with your character who does if he can experience these emotions with him.

Take out the exercise you worked on for the assignment in Day 6. Here, you were asked to explore the emotions of your characters and describe these emotions without naming the emotions. Read through what you've written. Where were you able to convey emotions without explicitly stating what the character was feeling? What kind of physical impulses and sensations convey emotions? Assessing your own work with a critical eye is the best way to learn from your mistakes and avoid making them again in the future.

Here's a quick quiz.

DIRECTIONS: Next to each of these lines of physical description, write down what kind of emotion you think the character was experiencing.

1. He gritted his teeth until his jaw ached.

2. She felt her heart rise into her throat, making it difficult to breathe.

3. Her palms were so sweaty, she was afraid to take his hand for fear that he would notice.

4. His bottom lip began to quiver as the doctor told him the news.

HERE IS THE ANSWER KEY:

1. He was angry.

2. She was upset.

3. She was nervous.

4. He was sad.

Now, can't you see how describing the physical sensation brought on by the emotion is more rhetorically effective than describing the emotion itself? As readers, we connect with emotion only through a shared experience of knowing how it feels. If you make your readers *feel* what your characters feel by making them *experience* what your characters are experiencing, you'll have created a scene that resonates.

Write a minimum of two internal scenes from Act Two of your outline, scenes that stand out particularly for the range of emotions your character experiences. Perhaps your character wants something but can't have it. Or perhaps he's just learned some devastating news. Or perhaps he's in love with his brother's wife. Write both of these scenes, paying particular attention to conveying your character's emotions through physical description. If this scene includes dialogue, you may want to pay particular attention to what is being said versus what is being thought. Can you give your reader access to the indirect thoughts of your character? Consider, too, how setting can contribute to the mood of your character.

A final reminder à la Oscar Wilde's advice: While it's important to include emotion in your work, don't be totally humorless. Readers can instinctively tell the difference between earned emotion and sentimental drivel. It's healthy for a creative writer to cultivate a certain amount of humor in his work—even if you are writing dramas.

WEEK 7 ASSIGNMENT 4: *A Meditation on Theme*

For this final assignment of the week, I want you to think about something we haven't discussed much up to this point: Theme. The theme of your novel is basically the broad-sweeping, universal idea(s) you want to get across to your reader. For example, in *The Great Gatsby* some possible themes might be the emptiness of material wealth, or the "real" definition of the American dream, or the awful repercussions of obsessive love and/or marital infidelity. A single novel can have more than one theme, of course, but it shouldn't be limitless.

But a theme is just what a reader takes away from her own reading of the novel, you say. Cue the buzzer. Bzzzzzz. Wrong. You must have an idea of your novel's theme in the back of your mind as you write; this will help you come up with specific imagery, metaphors, or motivations that forward your plot. Is your theme the vileness of greed spawned from desperation? Perhaps your protagonist's conflict comes from a landlord, a scrawny old man from Texas, nickel-and-diming him out of his final deposit, accusing him of not dusting above the window frames. While this may not be a major scene in your novel, it could help underscore, in a subtle way, the major themes of your work.

On a piece of paper right now, I want you to write down the theme or themes of your novel. Spend some time reading through your outline and/or skimming the scenes you've already written. It's important that you actually take the time to write your themes down—don't simply do the work in your head. Again, while you may think you can take a shortcut and save some time by simply thinking through this task, remember the way we process information in our heads is often different from how we process the information on paper. And the reader—fortunately? unfortunately?—is never granted an all-access pass into our minds.

After you've brainstormed the major or developing themes of your novel, take out your outline again. From

Week 7

your outline, select one scene that could be used to reveal a bit of your theme. Write this scene, paying particular attention to the details, imagery, figurative language, actions, dialogue, and so forth that can help further or deepen one of your major themes. Remember, though, you don't want to be too obvious. So if that landlord is trying to nickel-and-dime your protagonist, don't have your character think: "Oh, that vile landlord. Greed, spawned from desperation, is a scourge on humanity!" Themes are best when treated in a subtle manner and not shoved down the throats of your dear readers. You should trust your readers to be smart enough to get it. Convey theme, instead, through a symbolic setting, a sharp or unique character trait, a minor character, or a bit of physical description. As an author you should never, ever, ever explicitly state your theme. (Remember the show-don't-tell rule.) Instead have your readers experience themes firsthand.

STUCK IN THE MIDDLE WITH YOU

Here you are, already more than halfway through your ninety-day writing challenge. You've only got forty days left to finish your draft! How do you feel about the progress you've made so far? If you've kept up with your assignments, you're probably astounded with the progress you're making. I hope this is the case. In fifty short days, you've written a substantial chunk of your novel, which is quite a bit more *actual writing* than you ever did when you just *talked* about writing a novel. You may feel like this writing schedule has been a bit like boot camp at times. I mean, *every day* you've had to write. I've taken no mercy on you, either, and I told you there'd be no room for complaining about being tired, cold, hungry, bored, or uninspired, etc. I feel a bit badly about that, even though I've known all along it's for your own good. So let's try a new method for just a moment. Before you move on to this week's work, I'd like you to do one short exercise. First, extend your right arm in front of you. Now bend your arm at the elbow, with palm facing toward you. Now, I'd like for you to reach over and gently pat yourself on the back for all your hard work. There you go. Doesn't that feel good?

Now back to work, buster! Forty days to go, and we're still in Act Two. Get going, pokey. The novel won't write itself.

Last week all of your scene writing was accomplished with an eye toward developing the internal life of your characters. And because characters are the most important aspect of your novel—everything, after all, hinges on them, their desires, their actions, and their motivations—creating an interior life is crucial to the success of your book. Think, for example, of a book like *Johnny Got His Gun*, a 1939 antiwar novel by Dalton Trumbo. In this book, the protagonist, a badly injured soldier, "had no legs and no arms and no eyes and no ears and no nose and no mouth and no tongue." Left with only his conscious mind, Johnny's entire life takes place internally. And that's quite a challenge for a novel.

However, even in a novel where the protagonist is trapped inside his own mind, Johnny finds a way to communicate with the outside world. By the end of the novel, a character who a reader initially thought would be stuck only with his own interiority eventually finds a way to talk to his doctors and nurses, by tapping Morse code with his head onto the pillow. The internal struggles of the disfigured Johnny then become external as he engages with the world around him. (Don't worry; I won't tell you how it ends—but it's not pretty.)

This novel serves as an excellent example for crafting and drafting Act Two of your novel. Even if you've never read *Johnny Got His Gun*, the takeaway point is this: You *must* engage your character in communion with other characters. There's a whole big world out there, even in the fictional realm. Make sure your characters are a part of it. One of the worst rookie mistakes you can make as a first-time novelist (or a second-time or a veteran) is the failure to connect your characters to the people around them by making the novel entirely too much about the interior life of your character. Have you ever read a book or watched a movie where you felt like nothing happened? Did you enjoy spending your time either reading or watching nothing happen? If I were a betting woman, I'd again wager: probably not. Remember Flannery O'Connor's sentiment: In a story, something happens.

This week, your assignments will be focused on crafting your external scenes of Act Two. Remember, if the overall purpose of a scene is to forward the plot, quicken the pace, or narrate action, the scene is primarily external, even if through the course of the scene some important, interior elements of your characters are conveyed. Act Two should contain plenty of conflict, plenty of yearning, and plenty of obstacles between your character and what she wants. Hopefully, because you spent so much time earlier assessing your outline, all these elements are already in place. If not, I'd suggest going back and revising your essay. Points off and a serious tsk-tsk for not completing your work on time.

Now take another look at Act Two of your outline. Which external scenes will require a dialogue scene? Which ones will rely on action? Which scenes are the most important in terms of forwarding your plot? Label these scenes accordingly. If you have no dialogue scenes or action scenes in your current outline, where might you fit some in? Act Two should contain a nice balance of both interior scenes and exterior scenes to give your reader an idea of how your character thinks when he's alone *and* how he acts in front of company.

Week 8

WEEK 8, ASSIGNMENT 1: *Lights, Camera, Action!*

An action scene is a common type of external scene that engages your character with the fictional world that surrounds him. Perhaps it's more useful to think about action scenes as those scenes in which characters are reacting to the events that are unfolding before them. How your character reacts depends on what she wants within the scope of the novel, and what it is she yearns for. Remember, you want the action of the novel to unfold organically, according to the desires, personality, and motivations of your characters. Refer back to your character bios as you draft your external scenes. According to the biographical sketch you've drawn of your character, how would your protagonist naturally react in such a situation? It's unlikely that a devout nun would steal the high school mascot (a llama) at her fifteen-year high-school reunion, then drink beer in the old teacher's lounge before having a one-night stand with the old quarterback of the football team. That is, unless she only became a woman of the cloth in order to recover from the unexpected breakup from her high school boyfriend, the old second-string quarterback. Doh! Every decision she makes seems to revolve around that silly high school romance. Now that'd be a story!

At this point, it's important to note that as you're writing, your character may have a tendency to react in a way that differs from how you originally envisioned it on your outline, and this is okay. Go with what feels natural to you, and revise your outline as necessary. Remember, outlines should not be considered restrictive, but rather guideposts that give you a sense of direction along the way. Hopefully, since you did much of the thinking through of this novel weeks ago, you've freed up some mental space that will allow you to keep filling those pages.

The pacing of an action scene is often quick and should reflect the nature of the action being narrated. As a result, your readers tend to read these pages quickly, trying to keep up with the events unfolding before their eyes. Here are some general rules to keep in mind when writing an action scene:

- Always begin an action scene in *medias res*—in the middle of the action. Your reader should feel like they are already immersed in the action at the start of the scene. Consider these two examples. Which one captures your immediate attention as a scene-opening sentence?

  Example One: Gil swallowed the cyanide capsule.

  Or

  Example Two: Gil opened the cabinet, then looked at himself in the mirror. He had to go to the bathroom first. Once he was finished, he washed his hands and picked up the vial. He opened it, shook the pill into his hand, took a deep breath. Finally, after waiting a while, Gil swallowed the cyanide capsule.

Hopefully, you were more drawn in by the immediacy of the first example. You are immersed in the action of the scene immediately by the first short, sharp line that immediately gets to the point. Remember, one goal of an action scene, in addition to forwarding your plot, is to get your reader quickly turning pages. Trust me, a reader loves the feeling of getting through a chapter, or even a section of pages, quickly. Perhaps it's merely psychological, but turning pages makes a reader feel like progress is being made, if not by the storyteller, then by the reader herself.

- Include as many sensory details as possible in action scenes. What does your protagonist hear, feel, smell, taste, or see? Narrating the physical sensations as your character is experiencing them will help your readers feel like they're part of the action, too. Your reader needs to experience the action along with your characters.

- Avoid long, lengthy descriptions of setting or interior monologues. It is unlikely that your character will stop to think about how beautiful the setting sun is while he's being chased by two drug thugs with AK-47s. Remember, action scenes should reflect the pacing of the actions being narrated. Long paragraphs of exposition will slow your reader down. Think: pacing, pacing, pacing.

- Make sure you show how your character reacts to the actions within the scene. While the reader doesn't want a paragraph of rumination, a few precise details will help us know what is going on in the mind of your character and what the consequences of the actions will be. Is Gil scared at the moment? Does he think about his kids? What is the last thought he has before popping that pill?

- Think of the best way to end the scene: a cliff-hanger? Will Gil survive the cyanide poisoning? A revelation? Gil's wife swapped the cyanide out with beef bullion cubes, and now he has a case of particularly meaty burps? Either way, the consequences of your action scene should extend beyond the scene itself.

Now review each of your action scenes from Act Two of your outline and write them, keeping in mind the general rules above. (Do not focus yet on the climax scene or the scene that immediately precedes the climax; we'll be working on these later.) These types of scenes are the most tactile scenes in your novel, so be certain you are writing with the senses. What does your character see, smell, think, feel, hear? Be sure to pay attention to pacing and to starting as close to the conflict as possible. Don't make your reader wait too long for something to happen. If you do, she might fall asleep waiting.

WEEK 8, ASSIGNMENT 2: *Talk It Out*

All novels must have dialogue because it's important to let your character speak in his or her own words. Back on Day 7, we reviewed some of the fundamental rules for dialogue, and you practiced writing some dialogue scenes of your own. One thing to remember about a dialogue scene is that it doesn't simply contain the words that the characters are speaking. You'll also need to narrate the setting, the body language of your character, action, and descriptions. Dialogue scenes aren't just conversations but conversations that go somewhere and add to the overall trajectory of your novel.

Many of your scenes will contain small bits of dialogue, but scenes that contain a good amount of dialogue, or are composed entirely of swaths of dialogue, should come into play in your novel as well. Like action scenes, dialogue scenes are useful for quickening the pace of your novel. But keep in mind, dialogue scenes aren't simply scripted blocks of spoken texts. Instead you should be sure to fold in your direct lines of dialogue with descriptions of action, body language, and movement. What else are your characters doing besides talking?

Take a look at this excellent example from Richard Russo's novel *Nobody's Fool*. As you read, pay attention to how the dialogue is punctuated, how lines of speech are intertwined with expository narration, and how the author forwards the scene through this conversation.

> The men on the trailer steps watched several of these aborted attempts, shaking their heads in good-humored disbelief. Sully and Will watched for a moment also, the boy's eyes growing wide and round with wonder and fear.
>
> "What's wrong with him, Grandpa?" the boy asked.
>
> "He had a little accident a couple weeks ago," explained Sully, who had seen the dog a couple of times in the interim. "You want to ride on my shoulders?"
>
> When Will nodded enthusiastically, Sully swung him aboard.
>
> "Look who's here," Carl Roebuck said when he noticed Sully and the boy approaching. "You come to admire your handiwork?"
>
> "It's not my fault you got a spastic Doberman," Sully said, setting Will down on the step. The boy was still warily watching Rasputin circle. Hearing Sully's voice, the dog was now emitting small howls of frustration.
>
> "I think it *is* your fault," Carl said. "I just wish I could prove it." Then, to the two men who were watching the dog, "I know you guys'd love to stay here all afternoon and watch this dog have another stroke…"

"I would," one of the men said. "I admit it." But he and the other man headed for the gate, and Carl and Sully and the boy went inside the trailer.

Carl Roebuck went around behind the small metal desk and sat down, put his feet up and studied first the boy, then Sully. "Don Sullivan," he said knowingly. "Thief of Snowblowers, Poisoner of Dogs, Flipper of Pancakes. Secret Father and Grandfather. Jack-Off, All Trades. How they hangin'?"

Sully took a seat. "By a thread, as usual," he said. He motioned for Will to go ahead and sit on the sofa. "Don't ruin that," he warned.

Will looked at the sofa fearfully. It was torn to shreds, stuffing exploding from slits in the upholstery. Will climbed on carefully and found both men grinning at him.

"Your grandfather tell you how he poisons dogs?"

Will's eyes got big again.

"He steals people's snowblowers, too."

"Don't pay attention to him," Sully said. "He just can't keep track of his possessions."

Russo does an excellent job seamlessly integrating dialogue into this scene and allowing the conversation to flow, even as the characters move around. Importantly, Russo does not begin this scene with a line of dialogue, but instead offers up enough context in order to orient the reader as to who is doing the talking. Also note how Russo allows body language to do the "talking" when necessary. Will nods his head when he wants to ride on his grandpa's shoulders—this stands in place of a more contrived line like, "Yes, I do, Grandpapa." Later, Will's eyes get big instead of directly answering the question posed by Carl Roebuck. Any time body language can stand in the place of a direct line of dialogue, you should let it. Body language *is* a kind of language after all, and so it can communicate just as well what your characters are thinking as the spoken word can. It also provides a bit of action and momentum.

Also pay attention to Russo's dialogue tags. He never tries to get fancy with them. In your own dialogue scenes, aim for simplicity in your attributive tags. A simple "he said" or "she asked" will do; you never want to draw attention to dialogue tags by getting too creative (example: "he articulated loquaciously"). Remember, your aim is for invisibility when it comes to assigning lines of dialogue to a speaker. You want your reader to simply skim over the "he said/she said," using them only to discern who is speaking.

Another lesson we can learn from Russo's scene: The characters often speak in fragments, not complete sentences. Although you may have learned in elementary school to always write in complete sentences, dialogue is a different beast altogether. People don't always talk in complete sentences, and neither should your fictional characters. At least, not always. It's okay for your characters to interrupt one another, stop midsentence, or speak in short fragments.

Finally, and perhaps most importantly, Russo narrates action in the midst of the conversation between characters. Carl, Sully, and Will walk into a trailer. Carl then walks to a desk, sits down, and puts up his feet. Sully sits down. Will climbs on the couch. All these details are important because nobody has a conversation standing completely still. Unless he is a British beefeater guarding Buckingham Palace. And beefeaters don't speak. At least not while on duty. (I'm sure they yammer on during their off hours when they go to the local pub to knock back a few pints.)

Before moving on to your assignment, I'd like you to take out the dialogue scenes you wrote for Day 7. Give yourself an honest grade from 1 to 10 (1 being the worst, 10 being the best) on how well you did in this exercise. Practice being your own best critic. What tips can you take from Russo's scene above? What could you have done better? It's a good idea to learn from your practice exercises before moving on to the real thing.

Once you've assessed your work, comb through the scenes in Part Two of your outline and write any scenes that are primarily conversations. (Once again, do not yet focus on the climax or the scene before the climax.) Be sure to integrate action, descriptions of setting, and descriptions of your characters' body language. Be sure, also, to review the tips for crafting dialogue from Day 7.

Once you've written these scenes, read them aloud. Trust me, the best way to catch stilted, unbelievable dialogue is to read it out loud. If it doesn't sound real, it probably won't read much better either.

WEEK 8, ASSIGNMENT 3: *The Scene Before the Scene*

F. Scott Fitzgerald once wrote, "Action is character." I've always liked this quotation because I think it speaks to the distinction—or shall I say similarities—between plot-driven novels and character-driven novels. All action is representative of your character (and his desires/motivations/yearnings), and therefore the plot of your novel is also going to represent some aspect of character, too. Plot and character are, by definition, intrinsically linked.

Many writers, myself included, have a tendency to create a plot based on what sounds interesting, peculiar, compelling, comical, or exciting to them, without considering what this means to the character formation of the novel's major players. Maybe I want to write a scene where a

Christmastime mall elf gets fired for stealing candy canes because I think this is a funny story. However, if this scene has nothing to do with the rest of my plot, and if this does nothing to develop the character of my main players, this scene should not be included. That's the trick of novel writing, balancing the micro (the scene) and the macro (the novel). You must always look in two places at once.

Aristotle once said "The plot, since it is the imitation of an action, must confine itself to one complete action alone. The structure of the parts must be so interrelated that, if any one of them is moved or taken away, the whole plot will be distorted." In other words, all "parts" of your novel, every scene, must have a specific purpose and function within the scope of your overarching plot. We can apply this thinking to our own novels by simply asking ourselves, "Is this scene necessary?" Although we will be spending more time in a later week thinking about revision and editing techniques, you should always be aware—as you are writing—of the purpose and necessity of each of your individual scenes. I want you to take a look at the scenes you've written so far for Act Two. Spend some time skimming each scene and ask yourself, "What would happen to my novel if I deleted this scene?" If you took away the scene, would the "whole plot be distorted," as Aristotle notes? Does the scene highlight an important aspect of your plot or of your characters? If not, you'll be forced to either raise the stakes in the scene or delete it altogether. Bye-bye candy cane–stealing mall elf. See you in another story. Maybe. Or maybe not. Not every word we pen is fit for public consumption. You need to get FDA approval first, i.e., Final-Draft Adequacy.

Next week we'll focus on the climax scene of your novel. In the final assignment for this week, however, I want to focus on the scene that leads into your climax scene; that is, the scene directly preceding it. If you've ever played volleyball, you know the general principle of play: bump, set, spike. The bump brings control back to the ball, stabilizes it; the set, prepares and positions the ball perfectly for that final ... SPIKE. The spike is, of course, the real power play, but one that would be impossible without the bump and the set. Your novel's first two acts are a bit like the bump and the set in volleyball. All the work you've done so far has prepared your reader for the big power play—the climax. It's important that your lead-in to the climax scene be set just right. (Have you ever seen a player attempt a spike on a ball that's been poorly set? Have you ever seen a set from a ball that's been poorly bumped? It's a mess! And I should know. I played fourth string on the high school volleyball team until, thinking better of it, they made me the team statistician. I watched a lot of bumping, setting, and spiking.)

Spend just a few minutes reviewing your climax scene as noted on your outline. If, by this point, you think your climax scene has changed, do the necessary work editing your outline. Don't focus too much on the particulars of the climax, as we'll spend time on your climax scene next week. But it's important by this point to at last have some vague idea of how this scene will take shape.

In the traditional structure of a novel (and, of course, there are always exceptions to the rules), you'll find exposition, rising action, climax, falling action, and a conclusion.

Right now I want you to look at the scene that immediately precedes your climax. This is the final scene of the rising action.

According to Aristotle, these scenes must be so interrelated that to remove one will distort the other. Why did you choose this scene? If the climax is the scene that dramatizes the major themes and tensions of your novel, how can you use the scene before to set up this drama? What hints can you give your reader of the drama to come? Remember, the climax scene is the boiling point of your novel—what happens in the scene directly before to exacerbate the problems for the protagonist? What is the "final straw" that leads to the climax scene—you know, the one that broke that camel's back?

Now write this scene. Keep in mind that this scene immediately precedes your climax, the highest emotional-stakes scene in your novel. While you want to build up to this scene, you also want to be sure you don't have two too similar scenes back to back. Think about what you want your climax scene to look like and work backward from there. How can you slowly build the tension? What subtle hints can you give about what might happen next? How can you develop themes through imagery, symbolism, or figurative language? What techniques that we've learned can you use to quicken the pace? Remember: balance. Remember: beginning, middle, and end. Remember: Keep writing, keep filling pages.

ON THE OTHER SIDE OF A BRIDGE TOO FAR

The thing about habits, in general, is that once you've established them, you hardly notice them at all. Think of all the habits or routines that are incorporated into your daily life: Every morning and evening (at least, I hope) you brush your teeth without blinking an eye. If you're like me, your morning routine also always involves brewing a strong pot of coffee. (Please don't bother me until then.) If you've got a bad habit, maybe you don't even notice when you are biting your nails because it's become second nature to you. (I used to share an office with an individual who would leave nail slivers on our shared desk. Gross.)

About two months ago your writing habits were likely different. Maybe you always put writing off until you found the time to really focus on it—only to realize that you were never affording yourself any writing time at all. Or maybe you procrastinated because it seemed so daunting to write an entire novel, even though it's something you've always wanted to do. Now, after almost two months, you can confidently say your writing habits have improved. Have you found that it's a little bit easier to carve out the time to write? Are people (mostly) respecting your ninety-day challenge, allowing you the space and time to write? Have you found that you're actually eager to return to your writing desk each day? Maybe you don't even think about it anymore. You just automatically navigate to your writing nook after the dinner plates are cleared.

Perhaps you've developed other habits, too. Maybe you put on a writer's hat—literally. I used to write wearing my favorite blue baseball cap because I honestly thought the brim of the hat directed my focus forward—and toward my computer screen. It was a bit like those blinders used on horses. Maybe your habits are different: You always write wearing one red sock and one green one. Or you simply must sip a cup of coffee out of your favorite chipped mug while you write. Maybe you like to listen to Gregorian chants as you write, finding the rhythmic mantras soothing somehow. The fact of the matter is, it doesn't matter *how* you write, it matters *that* you write. Hopefully, this is a lesson you've learned by now: You can use any trick in the book to force yourself to write—bribes, incentives, rituals. But at the end of the day, if you don't produce the words, it doesn't matter how close you were to getting it done. Harsh, perhaps. True, certainly.

At this point in your novel-writing process, you should be feeling pretty good about your progress. You've written your first scenes that helped the reader get to know your character in Act One and some "internal" and "external" scenes that deepened your novel's plot in Act Two. Throughout the process you've been looking for ways to deepen the conflict from your main character—to extend your character's yearning. This work is, of course, all leading to one place: the climax.

WEEK 9, ASSIGNMENT 1: *Mountaintop Messages*

At the end of Act Two, the tension you've been building up to this point needs to come to a head. Think back again to the structure of a novel we discussed in an earlier section: A traditionally structured novel contains exposition (or rising action), followed by the complication (or nouement), culminating in the crisis (or climax), followed by the falling action that leads to a resolution (denouement). The crisis moment, or climax, located on the diagram at the tip of the mountain, is the defining or key scene in your novel—the moment of "realization" after which nothing can ever quite be the same for your protagonist. It is the point of no return. Your character must be changed in some fundamental way by the climax scene: She must turn and face the world an altered individual, and she must deal with a new reality, the product of the fallout of the climax scene.

You all know the fairy tale *Snow White*. Snow White's poor mother dies in childbirth, and she's left to the care of her jealous, wicked, egomaniacal stepmother, the queen. (Can you find me an example in the canon of fairy tales where a stepmother is not wicked?) As you know, this particular wicked stepmother is obsessed with looking in the mirror, asking it, "Who is the fairest one of all?" She grows angry when she learns that Snow White is the fairest, so she devises a plan to kill her. The huntsman in charge of killing her, of course, takes pity on this beautiful princess and leaves her in the woods, where she lives with those dwarves. Later, when the queen asks her mirror her favorite question, she learns that Snow White is still alive. Commence attempted murder.

Think for a moment about the climax of this well-known fairy tale. At what moment can nothing be the

Week 9

same for the protagonist, Snow White? It's a tricky question because Snow White faces so many obstacles, not the least of which is attending to the household needs of seven little people. But at what point in the story must all characters in the story turn and face a new reality, recognizing that the consequences of the climatic event will change their lives forever?

Some might guess that the climax moment is the very moment Snow White is banished to those creepy woods; after all, she can't go home, and that's quite a change. Others might guess it's when the evil stepmother asks that omniscient beauty-monitoring mirror if she is now the fairest (because she believes Snow White to be six feet under). Others might guess it's when Snow White dumbly bites into that crisp, poisoned apple. However, these moments are not quite the ones when Snow White is faced with a decision of consequence. Remember, the climax is the turning point of the entire story, a moment of realization that life cannot go on as is. The story has given us many conflicts: jealousy, vanity, and murder (or complicity to attempted murder). What is the final turning point in the story? What is the final crisis when there is no going back, not for anyone, and a "new normal" will have to be established?

It is precisely at the moment that Snow White's red lips are kissed by that handsome prince that the story is reversed. Snow White wakes up, and someone's going to be royally ticked off. No longer can she serve as an indentured servant to those dwarves. No longer will she sing "Whistle While You Work" so cheerily. She's found a man, ya'll! And now that vain step-ma will face her comeuppance. Will Snow White get married? Will the evil queen be served her just desserts? You'll find out in the resolution, which should answer these questions. Needless to say, this fairy tale ends on a happy note. Millions of children rejoice.

But not all endings conclude with such happiness and justice in the novelistic world. (And, keep in mind, a novel's climax-resolution will be much longer than a short story's.)

Let's consider the example of that old sport Gatsby again. Do you recall the climax of *The Great Gatsby*? At what point can nothing be the same for the characters in this novel? How about the point in the novel when Gatsby forces Daisy to tell Tom about their (re)union? (Gatsby always felt Daisy was rightly his somehow. Finders keepers!) After this point in Fitzgerald's tale, nothing will ever be the same—for any single character in the book—*because of* this "never should have happened" reunion. (Daisy admits at one point, after all the beans have been spilled, that she loves *both* her husband and Gatsby. But Gatsby's not satisfied with only half her heart.) Once everyone knows about the affair between Gatsby and Daisy, decisions are made, action is prompted. Fallout and chaos ensue. This is why the climax is often called the scene of recognition—everyone (the reader, too) realizes that they've crossed the bridge that's taken them too far from the starting point. They can't turn around; they can only move forward.

Take a look at your outline again and decide which scene will be your climax. Ideally, this scene will be one of the last scenes in Act Two or one of the first scenes in Act Three. In which scene has your character passed the point of no return? Is there one yet? You may want to ask yourself these questions:

- What is the defining moment in your novel for your protagonist? Why is this scene so important?

- At what point does your protagonist learn something about herself that makes it impossible to go back to the way things were?
- Have you adequately built up to this moment, revealing the importance of it?
- How is your character changed by this scene? How is this important to the novel as a whole?
- What will happen next? What will need to happen in order for your novel to be resolved?

The climax scene itself should be a balance between an external scene and an internal scene. And the reader should experience the scene along with your major players, so be sure to provide plenty of visceral detail. While the climax is the height of action within your story, it is also the scene with the most emotional tension. It is the scene with most at stake for your character. Don't forget the general rules for describing the emotions of your characters.

As we've discussed in a previous lesson, emotion is best conveyed through physical description. Instead of writing "Jeffrey was elated because he was made captain of his soccer team," you should describe what Jeffrey is physically feeling. Does his head feel like a balloon that's about to float away? Does his face hurt from smiling? What does he literally feel?

Remember Mark Twain's warning, which I'll repeat again: "The difference between the right word and the almost right word is … the difference between the lightning bug and the lightning." Be sure you're paying particular attention to word choice as you describe the emotions of your character in this scene. Paying attention to word choice can turn a mediocre scene into a sensational one.

But emotion can be conveyed in other ways, too. I'm sure you've heard the saying "Actions speak louder than words." And last week we discussed Fitzgerald's adage that "Action is character." How your character acts will say something about your character, too. This may seem an obvious point, but it's one worth considering in your climax scene. For example, when Jeffrey finds out he's team captain, what does he do? Break up with his girlfriend and buy a BMW on his mom's credit card? Does he say a private prayer, "Thanks, G!"? Does he do cartwheels and dance around the room? Does he pretend he's a wolf and begin howling at the moon? It's important you make the right decisions, decisions that arise organically from your character. Again, you might want to keep you character bios handy, just in case you need reminders about your characters' motivations.

Yet another way you can convey emotion is by including a flashback scene. Flashing back to a scene that takes place prior to your novel's present time can often reveal *why* the climax scene is so important to your character. By comparing the past to the present, you can often convey an unspoken internal tension.

Consider this example from Margaret Atwood's haunting dystopian novel *The Handmaid's Tale*:

> I don't feel like a nap this afternoon, there's still too much adrenaline. I sit on the window seat, looking out through the semisheer of the curtains. White nightgown. The window is as open as it goes, there's a breeze, hot in the sunlight, and the white cloth blows across my face. From the outside I must look like a cocoon, a spook, face enshrouded like this, only the outlines visible, of nose, bandaged mouth, blind eyes. But I like the sensation, the soft cloth brushing my skin. It's like being on a cloud.

They've given me a small electric fan, which helps in this humidity. It whirs on the floor, in the corner, its blades encased in grillework. If I were Moira, I'd know how to take it apart, reduce it to its cutting edges. I have no screwdriver, but if I were Moira I could do it without a screwdriver. I'm not Moira.

What would she tell me, about the Commander, if she were here. Probably she'd disapprove. She disapproved of Luke, back then. Not of Luke but of the fact that she was married. She said I was poaching, on another woman's ground. I said Luke wasn't a fish or a piece of dirt either, he was a human being and could make his own decisions. She said I was rationalizing. I said I was in love. She said that was no excuse. Moira was always more logical than I am.

Even if you have never read *The Handmaid's Tale*, you can see from this brief excerpt how flashback is used to draw out the conflicted inner workings of the narrator. The scene begins in the present moment. Then the narrator thinks back to her friend Moira who once disapproved of the narrator's burgeoning relationship with a married man. You can tell, simply from context, that the narrator is comparing the situation she's in now (with the Commander) to her past relationship with Luke. Atwood seamlessly shifts from past to present in this novel, using flashback as a writer's tool for examining the interiority of her protagonist.

Yet another way to reveal internal tension in the climax scene is through the setting. How does the setting reflect your character or the scene? How does the way the character observes the setting reveal something about what he's thinking or feeling? After learning he's the captain of the soccer team, does Jeffrey notice the torn couch cushions in his house or the sun shining brilliantly outside his basement apartment? Ask yourself how you would feel if you just achieved something meaningful to you. What would be the range of your emotions? What would be the first thing you'd think of—the fact that your parents will be proud or the fact that all the girls will want to date a captain of the soccer team or the fact that you'll have power over other team members?

Before you write your climax scene, ask yourself:

- What is the depth of my character's emotion in this scene? What is she feeling?
- What historical information about my character might be useful in conveying the importance of this scene to my reader?
- How will my character react to the plot point of the climax?
- How can you use setting to convey the mood or the tension of the scene?
- Is this climax scene important enough to affect change in my character?

Spend some time jotting down the answers to these questions before you begin writing your climax scene. And, yes, you should actually write the answers down, even if you only scratch them out on a note card. As I've said before, people tend to think through things differently in their heads than on paper. Be sure to spend an adequate amount of time developing this scene, pacing it, and drawing out the tension; this scene will naturally set you up for the rest of your novel. Or, if we return to our volleyball metaphor ... the SPIKE!

Here's another metaphor, if you prefer. Your readers will arrive at your climax scene after spending hundreds of pages, and many hours, hiking up that mountain of your novel with your characters. Once they get there, to the tip-top, they'd better have a spectacular view, or they're going to think they wasted their time, sweat, and energy climbing. Nothing worse than a getting to a place that was promised to be beautiful, only to find out it was bulldozed flat and turned into a strip mall.

Now get to work writing this climax scene, and spend plenty of time on it. Be sure to pay attention to how your character is both acting and reacting. Because this scene is such an important one, almost the entire week is dedicated to writing it. And remember, as Aristotle reminds us, each scene should be interconnected. If you find yourself going "off script" from your outline, it's perfectly fine. But be sure to go back to previous scenes and make the necessary edits and changes.

WEEK 9, ASSIGNMENT 2: *Adjusting the Picture*

The climax scene, and ensuing chaos, will cause some serious shifts to take place in your fictional world. What happens in your climax scene will basically dictate the terms of the rest of your novel—or at least hint at the possible plot outcomes. For example, revealing Daisy and Gatsby's relationship to Tom Buchanan caused 1.) Daisy and Gatsby to race off in Gatsby's car; 2.) Daisy, upset, to hit Myrtle with her car and never look back; 3.) Tom, also upset, to reveal whose car hit Myrtle (Gatsby's); 4.) Mr. Wilson, even more upset, to kill Gatsby in revenge for his daughter's death. Four rather significant plot points take place both *after* the climax and *because of* the climax. What kind of chaos does your climax cause? Think through this problem in a logical manner. Now write a list of all the outcomes resulting from your chaos. Adjust your outline accordingly. You may find yourself finishing this assignment before the week is up, and if this is the case, spend some time reworking some of your earlier scenes. Or, if you prefer, do something you haven't done in two months: Take a night off. (But only one.)

SO LONG, FAREWELL

Stop reading for a moment and stand up. Okay, now sit down. Okay, now stand up. Sit down, stand up, sit down. And one more time, stand up. Sit down. Are you following? Stand up, now sit. Stand up (with vigor this time! No slacking!). Now sit down. Stand, sit. Stand, sit. (Had enough yet?)

I could keep going on and on and on to demonstrate by proxy just how frustrating it is to the reader when he or she feels there is just no point to what the author is saying. I could keep having you stand up, then sit down just to demonstrate the *work* that reading a novel can sometimes feel like. You've put some real faith into an author any time you commit to reading her book. You're saying: *Hey, I most likely don't know you personally, but I trust you enough to spend several hours with you. Please use my time wisely!* And let's face it, the average individual has plenty of other things he could be doing: playing video games, watching movies, surfing the Internet, taking foreign-language classes, yo-yoing, learning to twirl a baton, etc.

At all points in your novel you need to respect your audience—even though you can't predict your audience. This is why we've been paying close attention to fictional elements large and small such as character nuance, convincing dialogue, and cohesive narrative arcs. Your reader is donating her time to you, gratis, and in return you must respect your reader enough to tell the best story you can. In no place is this respect more essential than in Act Three. Your reader has invested time and energy—yes, reading is energy (and fundamental!)—forgoing time spent cleaning, running errands, or hanging out with family and friends— and she wants to feel like the ending is worth the wait. And let's face it—you owe it to your characters, too. Characters you've spent hours creating, giving history and personality to. Characters you've given *life* to. (But don't get a god complex about it or anything.)

In the last lesson and assignment, you did a lot of the necessary work to set your novel up for the resolution: Act Three. In your climax scene, your character faced a turning point; he acted and reacted. He emoted. Now it's all downhill, baby! Right? Well, not exactly. Endings are never easy. You still have a lot of work ahead of you. But if you've consciously thought through some of the choices you've made in earlier scenes, Act Three will write itself. Well, sort of.

WEEK 10, ASSIGNMENT 1: *Bump, Set, Spike … Then What?*

Have you ever seen a movie that ended too abruptly? Just as the bad guy was caught, the screen went black, and the credits rolled. The problem with an ending like this is that the director failed to include enough "falling action" to give the movie a cohesive feel. The director didn't answer any of those "and what happened next" questions that the rising action or the climax scene of the film prompted. Moviegoers will leave a movie like this feeling dissatisfied, even if the movie was entertaining up until that quick-exit ending.

A novel that ends too abruptly is as equally dissatisfying. If your reader has hiked up that mountain of exposition and rising action with you, don't leave them stuck at the apex. You'll need to lead your reader back down from that mountaintop, at least partway. After the climax, life goes on in your fictional world. What does this life look like? What will be the "new normal" for your characters?

The scene following the climax scene, or the falling-action scene(s), should be treated a bit like a resting place for your readers, a time for them to pause, collect themselves, and assess the importance of what just happened in the scene they just read. Because your climax scene is—or should be—a high-stakes emotional scene, and because you want to avoid back-to-back dramatic/emotional scenes, it's a good idea for the scene immediately following your climax to be, shall we say, lower on the scale of emotional intensity. After the climax scene, the main character often steps back from the story to give a bit of necessary perspective. What is the remaining fallout from the climax scene? How has the protagonist's thinking changed from the beginning of the novel to the end? How has he been shaped by the events of the climax? Who is he now, and who does he want to be?

Lolita by Vladimir Nabokov and *My Ántonia* by Willa Cather, though very different novels (one is about a charming pedophile, the other is about a nostalgic Midwesterner), employ similar techniques in their respective "falling action" scenes. Both narrators, obsessed with and/or nostalgic for the women in their lives, return to visit their former flames years after the novel's climactic moment. Both narrators, now with the advantage of distance and time, are able to reflect on what these women have meant to them and how these women have changed them. The reader witnesses the deep longing both narrators feel for these women, and also the ways these narrators have evolved through the course of their experiences.

The scene following the climax should also, of course, answer some of the questions set up by the climax. If your narrator discovered that her husband and his secretary with whom he was having an affair were the ones who stole the half million dollars from the megachurch where they belonged, will she turn him in? Or begin planning a move to that big house for sale that she's always envied? Will she leave him? Will she blackmail him into staying with her instead of that cheap, blonde floozy? You're going to have to answer these questions for your reader. And, moreover, the answer to these questions will depend to a large degree on how you've set up your novel, how you envision your protagonist changing, and what you see as the ideal ending for the book.

If the climax dramatizes the themes of your novel, the scene immediately following the climax should underscore or reiterate this theme. But a word of advice: Don't be too obvious. That is, your reader can glean your intended message without your protagonist overtly explaining: "I have been changed dramatically by the events of the climax, and here's how." By this point in your novel, you've included several scenes that reveal the emotional core of your characters—and subtlety is often the best path to tread. Check yourself to make sure you aren't being too heavy-handed in the scene following your climax. Some good advice: Save the drama for your mama. (Apparently, mothers like drama.) Readers, however, don't want messages pressed upon them; instead they will be more satisfied if they feel they've arrived at these thematic connections on their own.

Write the scene that immediately follows your climax—the first falling-action scene—paying close attention to answering the "What next?" questions your climax gives rise to *and* to stepping back from the emotional/dramatic intensity of the previous scene. How do you plan to transition from the climax to this scene? What kind of perspective does your character have now? How has she evolved? Remember to address your character's internal state and external surroundings.

WEEK 10, ASSIGNMENT 2: *Tying Off Mini-Threads*

Act Three is often referred to as the *resolution*, but this term can be tricky since it denotes a positive finality, which is not often the case. If you *resolve* a problem, you are finding a solution to it, and some endings aren't quite as clear-cut in fiction. Many novels don't end on a happy note. Remember the varieties of endings we examined back on Day 16. Your character can either:

a.) Get what she wants.
b.) Not get what she wants.
c.) Get what she wants but realize that it was no longer important to her.
d.) Not get what she wants, but get something even better than what she wanted in the first place.

Often Act Three leaves the reader feeling cathartic, anxious, defeated, or even uncertain. You must remember, these are resolutions, too, even if nothing has been definitely resolved. Perhaps your character found the true identity of her father—only to discover something much worse, a family secret she wished had remained buried.

Think of our dear Gatsby again. How was this novel resolved? With a gunshot, I'm afraid. Gatsby dies in his pool, and the older-and-wiser narrator, Nick Carraway, now longs to return to the simplicity of his Midwestern roots as a consequence. He's seen the ugly side of wealth; he understands what a "voice full of money" can do to a man who hears it. We've already discussed the ways in which the climax of the novel leads directly to the final plot points in your fictional world, but you must also pay attention to what other mini threads of your narrative must be resolved. In *The Great Gatsby*, several mini threads are tied up at the novel's conclusion. For one, the reader learns of the great mystery of Gatsby's identity. Jay Gatsby was Jimmy Gatz, a man who tried to reinvent himself, and isn't this reinvention a big part of what the American Dream is all about? We learn that all those partygoers from earlier in the novel, all those people who populated Gatsby's lavish home, drank his booze, and took moonlight swims in his pool, really aren't his friends. None of them came to his funeral, and it's likely none of them will even miss the old sport. How sad would it be to spend your life in the company of people who don't really care about you? We learn that Nick breaks up with his sometimes girlfriend Jordan, and Daisy and Tom remain together, despite the marital infidelities committed by both parties.

Spend some time perusing your outline and spot reading through some of your scenes. By now you should have a good amount of work in front of you, so this may take an hour or more of skimming. Which plot points do you still need to resolve? Which loose ends need to be tied up? What is the outcome of the climax scene? And, importantly, how has your central character changed?

Then write any scenes (except for the last) that resolve these mini threads.

WEEK 10, ASSIGNMENT 3: *Good-Bye is the Hardest Word*

The final scene of a novel, or even a movie, often leaves the most lasting impression. Think of it as the end of a relationship—you always remember how you said good-bye. Was it fiery and brief? Long, sentimental, and drawn out? A confusing set of unreturned voice-mail messages? These last moments probably stuck with you long after you moved onward and, hopefully, upward.

While there is, of course, no magic bullet for writing your final scene, these pages should do the following:

- Connect in some way to the beginning chapter/scene. (This will add a feeling of cohesiveness to your novel.)

- Be slower in pace and reflective in tone.

- Show how your character has changed since the beginning of the novel and what she has learned.

- Imply what the character wants for the future. (In other words, if there were an epilogue, what might it say? Did Josephine go on to change her ways? Did she enroll in cosmetology school and finally quit obsessing about her father?)

In an earlier lesson, we took a look at the opening sentences of Alice Sebold's best seller, *The Lovely Bones*. Let's now take a look at how she concludes this novel. These final paragraphs, remember, are narrated by the novel's dead protagonist, Susie Salmon:

> But now let me tell you about someone special:
>
> Out in her yard, Lindsey made a garden. I watched her weed the long thick flower bed. Her fingers twisted inside the gloves as she thought about the clients she saw in her practice each day—how to help them make sense of the cards life had dealt them. ...
>
> Samuel walked out to Lindsey then, and there she was in his arms, my sweet butterball babe, born ten years after my fourteen years on Earth: Abigail Susanne. Little Susie to me. Samuel placed Susie on a blanket near the flowers. And my sister, my Lindsey, left me in her memories, where I was meant to be.
>
> * * *
>
> And in a small house five miles away was a man who held my mud-encrusted charm bracelet out to his wife.
>
> "Look what I found at the old industrial park," he said. ...
>
> "This little girl's grown up by now," she said.
>
> Almost.
>
> Not quite.
>
> I wish you all a long and happy life.

Here, the pacing of the novel slows considerably. Lines like "I watched her weed the long thick flower bed. Her fingers twisted inside the gloves ..." are more languorous details that seem to extend time, draw out the final pages. These paragraphs are reflective, too. Susie examines her family's obsession with her death—the way they were, for many, many years, unable to move on from it. But Susie notes that they're finally able to move forward now; her sister "left me in her memories...." Yet we also know Susie's not been totally relegated to the past: Lindsey has named her first daughter after her deceased sister: Little Susie.

The language and tone of these final paragraphs also connect to the first pages, where Susie was also directly addressing her audience. The baby was born "ten years after my fourteen years on Earth," which, not coincidentally, situates the novel's end ten years after those first moments narrated in the opening pages of the novel. In the end, Susie directly addresses her audience once more, bidding them adieu: "I wish you all a long and happy life." This seems a strange last line for a novel, but it is one that resonates and gives us the lessons of the novel: The dead are at peace, and so, too, should be the living.

Take a look at your outline's last scene. Will the tone be reflective? Will it show what your character has learned? Now reread your first scene. How can you connect the final scene to this one? Return to the twenty final lines you wrote for your assignment on Day 16. Are any of these lines strong enough, now that you've written most of your novel?

Endings are never easy, but they carry a certain amount of emotional weight. If your readers arrive at the final scene only to find a character who is not authentic to himself—or an ending that feels contrived and unnaturally out of place—they'll be disappointed. In other words, your ending must be earned. The final scene—and especially the final line—is your final opportunity to leave a lasting impression on your reader before she closes the book for good. How do you want her to remember your character? Think about fictional characters from your favorite novels that live on in your mind, and then find a couple of those novels and reread how the author ended the book. In some ways, your final words should be the strongest, the most poetic, because these lines will be the last ones your audience reads, and so the first they'll remember.

POP QUIZ

Do you know to which novel/author this very famous last line this belongs to: "So we beat on, boats against the current, borne back ceaselessly into the past"?

Week *10*

MIND THE GAPS

The last ten weeks have been work. Grueling work, at times, as you forced yourself to write day after day or night after night. Nobody said it'd be easy, and you entered the ninety-day writing challenge well aware of the obstacles you'd face. If you're still here on Day 71, however, I'm guessing you've found reward in the process, too. Isn't it great when we prove to ourselves that we are capable of doing more than we ever thought we could? Or maybe this process has been bittersweet for you, as you realize the only thing that has ever really stood in the way between you and your novel has been, well, *you.* This is a lesson every writer must learn at some point, especially those who claim to struggle with finding the time/mojo/money/energy/place/space (i.e., excuses) to write.

You now have a draft of your novel in your hands (or on your computer, as the case may be. Be sure to create backups, multiple backups!). Throughout the past couple of months, you've learned how to develop character and how to reveal externally what your character feels internally. Chances are, if you've come this far, you're going to complete your novel—and not just say you will. You've proven to yourself, and others, what it takes to be a *real* writer. You've become the textbook definition of a writer, in fact. You're now someone who writes. And habitually at that. Before you continue, I'd like for you to take a moment and congratulate yourself.

But don't pop the cork on your celebratory bottle of champagne just yet.

Your first instinct might be to print a copy of your work, run to Kinko's, and make enough copies for every friend and/or family member who has ever said they'd like to read what you've written. You'll stuff those warm copies in envelopes and, heck, overnight your manuscripts to these people so they'll have a copy first thing in the morning. You want to get your work "out there" in the world; you want readers. You're proud of yourself. You want to show that all that time in the writing zone was worth it. After all, you've done more than 99 percent of people who say "someday I'll write a novel" have ever done. You've written it!

Well, almost. In reality, it's more like a thin draft. There's a well-known writer's dictum: Great novels aren't written— they're rewritten. Translation: You may have written a draft of your novel, but you still need to revise it. Revisions make mediocre novels into good novels and good novels into great novels and great novels into classic novels.

What does this mean for you, exactly? Time to get to work again. (What'd you expect? This book is titled *90 Days to Your Novel*, not *70 Days to Your Novel*.) You still have twenty days to throw that celebratory party, but I wouldn't put the invitations in the mail just yet.

Instead it's time to return to the world of reality. Or, rather, to the world of fiction. Your novel-in-progress. And, yes, you can now call it a novel-in-progress and not just

Week 11

an outline or a jumble of scenes. You are the proud new owner of a body of work. If fact, if you want to do something very therapeutic, make a copy of your outline and burn it. Throw it in a bonfire and watch the flames shrink that paper to a gray crumble of ash. You're through with it now. Hasta la vista, outline.

At least, *that* outline. (Now, cue my demonic laughter … bwhahahaha.)

Yes, you have a draft of your novel, and, yes, you have every reason to be proud of your work, but it's likely that all of your scenes won't flow perfectly together at this point. You've been writing scene by scene by scene, which has been very productive; however, maybe your scenes don't quite gel with each other. Maybe you were distracted when you wrote one scene, and it has a different feel—a different tone—than the others. Perhaps you're lacking some transitions, or perhaps your scenes are out of order. It's likely that some scenes are missing altogether from your novel. This is normal, and you need not be alarmed. If you've come this far, I have every faith that you'll be able to trek through these next weeks. As every veteran writer knows, there is no such thing as good writing, only good rewriting.

This week's assignments, then, focus on filling in the gaps of your novel and making sure the parts form a cohesive whole.

WEEK 11, ASSIGNMENT 1: *Outline to Novel to Outline*

This entire ninety-day writing challenge began with an idea that was developed into an outline, and this outline, in turn, was developed into a novel-in-progress. Now I'm going to ask you to do something that might feel contrary to your way of thinking and to your concept of writing—

and maybe even to your understanding of fairness and order in the universe. But if you give it a chance, I'm sure you'll find this exercise both useful and illuminating.

What I'm asking you to do is ... wait for it ... turn your novel-in-progress into an outline. There, I said it: I want you to turn your novel into an outline.

[Silence. Chirping of crickets. More silence.]

Now I can hear you through this page already: *No way, Jose! I suffered through weeks of working from an outline, and you told me I could burn it. I'll tell you where you can put that outline....* Whenever I ask my writing students to outline something they've already written, they look at me like I've got a little green Martian protruding from my forehead, an alien holding a sign that reads *Suckers!* Once my students realize I'm serious, they level their eyes, and if they had a puffy cartoon cloud extended from their heads, it might read: "Grumble, grumble."

Really, the outline has been the unfair recipient of a bad reputation, and I politely ask that you show it a bit of R.E.S.P.E.C.T. You know what that means to me? Quite simply, it means you recognized that the main function of an outline is to help you logically think through the creative process. Logic and creativity *really do* go together, despite your initial assumptions about the pair. Creativity isn't about disorder and chaos and self-destruction—these are clichéd assumptions about creativity and the process surrounding its use. Creativity is more about taking the world apart and putting it back together again, bit by bit, in an authentic and original way. In fact, creativity makes order *out of* chaos. And, coincidentally, so does an outline. Unlikely cousins, the two.

Outlining your novel won't be as daunting or as difficult a process as it may first sound. What I'm essentially asking you to do is create a reverse outline that will help you assess the micro in terms of the macro—or the scene in terms of the aims of the novel itself. I want you to outline what you have *already* written. Once you outline what you've written thus far, it'll be much easier to see what is missing, what needs rearranging, and what works well as it stands now in your novel.

The first part of this assignment asks you to print out all the assignments you've written from Week 6 through now. These will be all the scenes that comprise your novel-in-progress. Next, I'd like you to arrange these assignments in the order they'd likely appear in your novel. (For the most part, you wrote your scenes in a linear fashion, aside from some of your scenes from Act Two.) After you've arranged your scenes, clearly label the first page of each scene chronologically: "scene one," "scene two," "scene three," etc. Finally, I'd like for you to find a quiet place, away from disturbances, and read your novel-in-progress all the way through, start to finish. Try to do this in one sitting, if at all possible. You may use a pen to make any marks in the margins indicating what's working and what's not. (Where did you grow bored, for instance? Where did you want more clarity?) But your focus for now should be simply to read and get a sense of how your novel fits together as it currently stands.

Once you finish, your next task is to reverse outline each individual scene, assessing the scene's major components. Break down the scene/scene type, POV, setting, characters involved, summary, scene intention, and relationship of the scene to the overall plot. Use the following as an example:

Scene/Type/ POV	Three; dramatic action scene
POV	Odessa
Setting	Lincoln Memorial, winter
Major Characters	Finn, Eli, and Odessa
Summary	Finn and Eli meet to make the drug exchange. Eli is nervous because this is his first foray into the drug-dealing world, but he's desperate since he lost his job at Whale World. He is about to marry Odessa, and he wants to buy her a nice house, so he needs some money. Odessa suspects Eli to be cheating because he's been so mysterious lately. She follows him from a distance to the moment, and catches him in the drug deal. Eli doesn't know that Odessa was watching.
Goal/Intention of Scene	To show Eli's desperation and Odessa's lack of trust. This scene is meant to build tension between the two.
Relation to Overall Plot	This scene is the reason Odessa calls off the wedding, but Eli doesn't know this. He thinks Odessa just doesn't love him anymore because he's lost his job.

Spend some time breaking down your scenes into components and assessing them. Once you are finished with your reverse outline, print it, reread it, and ask yourself the following questions:

- What scenes are still needed? What's missing?
- Which scenes fall in Act One, Act Two, or Act Three of my novel?
- Does my novel include enough characters? How many, total, are in my novel? Are there any characters I could cut or combine?

- Where can I deepen the conflict, heighten the drama, or raise the stakes for the characters?
- In which chapters do I reveal information about my character's history?
- Which scenes could be cut because you could not find a purpose or it did not relate to the overall plot?
- Do I have a variety of scenes? Internal, external, action, emotional, dialogue?
- Do I provide a setting for each scene?
- Have I provided adequate lead-up to my climax?
- Have I provided adequate falling action (or lead-up) to my conclusion?
- Do I maintain a consistent POV? Or does the POV shift? If so, will the reader be confused? Would it be better to use only one POV?

By assessing each scene of your novel, you'll be better able to figure out which scenes are working and which ones aren't, which ones are necessary, and which ones are extraneous and should be cut. Reverse outlining is a great tool for helping you fill in the gaps of your novel-in-progress so that you can paint a clearer picture for your reader.

This assignment is also going to force you to practice what will be an essential skill for you as a writer: becoming your own harshest critic. Read and critique your work *as a reader would*. Be honest with yourself, and allow yourself to veer from the original course when needed. Writing is an art form, and even manned with outlines and checklists galore, there is no perfect formula. Hemingway once advised writers to "Develop a built-in bullshit detector." And his advice couldn't be more spot on. If the writing process feels like a cakewalk—if you never feel frustrated because you can't get the scene "just right" or if you've never agonized over how a character might react to a certain revelation—you may just be a bit too easy on yourself.

After all, even expert chefs make bad meals. That's part of the creation process. But with a little bit of tweaking—less salt here, a dash more pepper there—the meal can go from "bleh" to "mmm" in no time.

Once you've finished your reverse outline, make a note of which scenes need to be reworked and which scenes need to be either added or deleted. One of the most difficult revision skills won't necessarily be deciding where to add scenes but deciding which scenes to cut. Writers often grow attached to scenes once they've been written; after all, you put a good amount of work into its development. However, simply because you intended for a particular scene to be included in your novel doesn't mean that it belongs. When I cut scenes, I save many of them in a file named "Deleted Scenes" on my computer, and, believe it or not, some of these scenes have found homes in totally different stories. Others, of course, will die a long and silent death in the "Deleted Scenes" folder, and this is okay, too. Not every scene that comes out of our minds is worthy of being read by the general public.

Write any additional scenes that are necessary for cohesiveness in your novel; rework others that need a bit of support or clarity. And don't forget: cut, cut, cut.

WEEK 11, ASSIGNMENT 2: *Between the Scene*

We briefly noted in an earlier section that soap operas offer us excellent examples about what *not* to do in a novel. Just as you're really getting into the scene about the unlikely

Week 11

MIND THE GAPS

connection between Francesca and Preston, who are about to make love on a bed of red rose petals, the scene cuts out rather abruptly, and suddenly you're on some seedy, dark dock in a shipyard with malevolent Beatrice, Preston's ex-wife who is now carrying his child due to Gigi's evil switcheroo of petri dishes at the fertility clinic. And then suddenly we're at the hospital with Steig and Monte. They've been in a motorcycle accident, and both have lost their memories (even though, strangely, neither sustained any bodily injuries). Yikes! Soap operas don't provide viewers with smooth transitions—they simply jolt the viewer back and forth from story line to story line to story line.

We've been writing in scenes for a majority of the past ten weeks because a novel is simply a series of scenes strung together. However, without the necessary transitions, your novel is going to feel like a disjointed compilation of scenes and not seamless, cohesive work.

Transitions, as we've discussed on briefly on Day 13 when we talked about narrative summary, serve two main purposes. They can:

1. Orient your reader to changes in time, location, or point of view.
2. Summarize what has happened "between scenes" so that you can cut irrelevant, uninteresting, or unnecessary information.

The first purpose is self-explanatory: Either between scenes or, more likely, as you begin each new scene, you're going to have to redirect your reader to changes that have taken place. If time has leapt forward, how much time? A year? A day? Two weeks? Two minutes? If you've changed locations, where is the reader now? Statesboro, Georgia?

Mt. Nebo, West Virginia? Portugal? A tunnel beneath the earth? If the POV character has flipped, how can you immediately alert your reader to this? Through voice? Description? A simple pronoun swap?

Remember a couple of months back when we discussed Alfred Hitchcock's observation "Drama is life with the dull parts taken out of it" in relation to scene versus summary? Transitions can also serve the purpose of the "dull stuff." What I mean by this is simple: You can summarize in a transition (or summary plus transition) what you don't want to actually narrate in a scene. So, to continue with our example above, Odessa takes a long drive after witnessing Eli make a drug deal. She stops to buy a strawberry milkshake. She uses the bathroom at the gas station where she fills up her tank. She visits the park that extends along the river. She stops to get a Diet Coke at the 7-Eleven. She visits the library and returns her overdue books. She goes to Starbucks and orders a sugar-free vanilla soy iced latte, tall. (She's very thirsty, can you tell?) When she gets home three hours later, Eli asks her where the heck she has been.

Do we need to narrate, scene by scene, where Odessa has been? Do we need to be with her, present at the scene, as she drops her overdue library books into the book return? Or when she fills up her car with gas or drinks all those beverages or, inevitably, visits the loo? The answer, of course, is no. If you want to begin the chapter after Odessa's witnessing of Eli dealing drugs back at their apartment, you can simply summarize where Odessa has been in the previous three hours:

> Odessa had been gone three hours when she returned to Eli's worried looks. She had driven along the river, run

some errands, but had been thinking the entire time: Eli sells drugs. Eli sells drugs.

Go back now and read the beginning of each of your scenes. Have you provided an appropriate transition? Can you summarize the beginning of your scene so you can start each scene closer to the action? Does the scene begin in a place that flows with where the previous scene left off?

If you're finding these questions difficult to answer, or, even worse, if you feel your novel has no flow from chapter to chapter, you're going to have to do some rewriting at this point. Think about how you can condense, summarize, and narrate what happened between the scenes. Keep in mind that this can be accomplished in a subtle manner, with temporal signals such as "A week later ..." or a simple descriptive phrase such as "After she parked the pontoon boat ..." or even a simple pronoun shift, if the POV is changing. Remember Occam's razor, another tool that comes in handy from time to time: The simplest solution is usually the right one.

QUICK STARTS, GRAND FINALES, AND UNIVERSAL MESSAGES

Less than two weeks remain of your ninety-day writing challenge. Don't fall short of the finish line. Although it may feel like you have a working draft of your novel, we still have just shy of two weeks remaining to tweak, adjust, trim, and polish your novel. And since you signed a contract with yourself two and a half months ago, you're obligated (to yourself) to see this project through. By this point, you might be excited to even have a draft *at all*. Let's admit it: Writing a novel is something you've wanted to do for as long as you remember. And now that you've got all these pages before you, you just want to get the thing out in the world, show your friends and family the reasons why you've been so reclusive lately, tucked away in the lonely corner of your writing nook.

Even the greatest writers spend tedious hours, days, months, and even years revising their work. F. Scott Fitzgerald, for example, is notorious for his revision tactics, revising *The Great Gatsby* up until the very last minute, even as it was lying in galleys at the publisher ready to be printed. Can you imagine what details might have been included or taken away in those final moments? Perhaps Fitzgerald revised Gatsby's familiar "old sport" from "old bud" or "old fart," and this was a detail that could have made all the difference. I'm just guessing, of course. You'll have to visit his collection of papers at Princeton University to be sure.

Hollywood is no stranger to the revision process either. David Milch, producer and writer for HBO's award-winning series *Deadwood*, is known as a perfectionist in his industry, editing, cutting, and revising the actors' lines right up until the moment he yells "Action!" Though it might be a struggle, as an actor, to learn all your lines under such conditions, the final product was authentic, polished, and compelling. David Simon, too, most famous for his work on the highly acclaimed series *The Wire*, similarly reworks his scripts during the shooting process, focusing more on the writer's craft than the craft of acting. (As well he should—without good writing, there would be no good acting.)

The main point is simple: You can't expect to get everything right on your first go around. This week, we'll be taking a closer look at some strategies for rethinking and reworking some of the crucial scenes of your novel.

WEEK 12, ASSIGNMENT 1: *In the Beginning (Again)*

Let's go back to the beginning. Your novel's beginning, that is. It's been some weeks since you've written this scene, and, hopefully, that time has given you some necessary practice and, in addition, clear perspective on why you made the decision to begin your novel where you did. Many people will tell you that the first scene of your novel is the most important, and I agree with this, up to a point. The first scene, even the first paragraph and the first line, will determine whether or not your reader, faced with thousands of books on the shelves of the bookstore, will buy your book. And why should they? You've done them no favors. At least not yet. The first line will determine if your reader will read your next line, and your next line, and so on. If you want a stranger to continue reading your book, in fact, to *pay* to read your book, you absolutely must grab her attention immediately.

Furthermore, the first scene of your novel must be one of your sharpest because this is often the scene agents and editors will look at when deciding whether or not they wish to read the rest of your novel. If your end goal is to ultimately publish your novel, this first scene is often the only chance you've got to convince an agent or editor that the rest of your novel is even worth a look. Editors and agents, after all, aren't the mythical creatures we sometimes imagine them to be. They've got stacks and stacks of manuscripts on their desks that they must get through before they can go home to their families and friends. Trust me, they'll read quickly, and you have only a few moments to engage their interest.

Before you continue, I want you to go to your bookshelf and select a novel, perhaps your favorite, though any novel will do. I simply want you to read the first two to three paragraphs. Don't skim; read closely. Now, what did you notice? How did that author immediately catch your attention? We've already talked in a previous lesson about what your first lines and first scene should try to accomplish. It's likely that the novel you selected started with a strong first line, followed by some descriptive sentences that piqued your interest. Or maybe the situation itself was compelling.

Together let's take a look at this excerpt from the first pages of the bestseller *Memoirs of a Geisha* by Arthur Golden:

> Suppose that you and I were sitting in a quiet room overlooking a garden, chatting and sipping at our cups of green

tea while we talked about something that had happened a long while ago, and I said to you, "That afternoon when I met so-and-so … was the very best afternoon of my life, and also the very worst afternoon." I expect you might put down your teacup and say, "Well, now, which was it? Was it the best or the worst? Because it can't possibly be both!" Ordinarily I'd have to laugh at myself and agree with you. But the truth is that the afternoon when I met Mr. Tanaka Ichiro really was the best and the worst of my life. He seemed so fascinating to me, even the fish smell on his hands was a kind of perfume. If I had never known him, I'm sure I would not have become a geisha.

How does this short paragraph engage your interest? Does it? It must engage somebody's interest, because it sold millions of copies in the United States alone. Yes, plural. Millions. How's that for encouragement to write the best opening you can?

There is no right or wrong answer, of course, and different readers will likely have various reasons as to why they felt their interest was captured in these first lines. Here are mine: First, the opening is very conversational. The narrator is speaking directly to me, it seems: "Suppose you and I," the narrator says, which makes me think: *Are you talking to me? You must be! Nobody here but the page and me. I'm so flattered you feel such levels of familiarity with me after only a few short sentences. Why, yes, I would love some green tea. Now go on….*

But beyond the feeling of familiarity, this paragraph also brings up several thought-provoking and contradictory statements. I want to ask: Just how can a single afternoon be the best *and* worst day of your life? But I don't have time to ask this question because before I know it, the author reveals that her meeting with someone named

Mr. Tanaka Ichiro had something to do with her being a geisha. (And aren't geishas, sort of, well, um ... there's no polite way to put this: hookers?) That's a lot of information in one paragraph, and many readers, such as those millions of people who bought and read the book, agree: That's quite a hook. The significance of this starting point becomes obvious in the first pages of this novel: We are going to learn how Sayuri Nitta, the narrator, became a geisha and what her life as a geisha was like.

Let's take a look at one more example from a popular, oft-taught novel. Here are the opening paragraphs of Harper Lee's iconic *To Kill a Mockingbird*, a novel assigned in just about half of the high school classrooms across the country. Certainly, we can learn something from these opening paragraphs:

> When he was nearly thirteen, my brother Jem got his arm badly broken at the elbow. When it healed, and Jem's fears of never being able to play football were assuaged, he was seldom self-conscious about his injury. His left arm was somewhat shorter than his right; when he stood or walked, the back of his hand was at right angles to his body, his thumb parallel to his thigh. He couldn't have cared less, so long as he could pass and punt.
>
> When enough years had gone by to enable us to look back on them, we sometimes discussed the events leading to his accident. I maintain that the Ewells started it all, but Jem, who was four years my senior, said it started long before that. He said it began the summer Dill came to us, when Dill first gave us the idea of making Boo Radley come out.

Why do you think Lee decided to begin her novel at this particular moment? And, in addition, how do you think these two short paragraphs quickly engage the interest of the reader? Again, there is no right or wrong answer. Think about it for a moment. How can you apply these techniques to your own work?

In this passage, Lee is using a short description of a familiar incident (the broken arm) in order to segue to the "real" starting point of her novel, the summer Dill comes to Maycomb. This is the same summer that Jem and Scout (narrating now several years from the novel's main events) become obsessed with trying to get Boo Radley to "come out." What natural questions will arise from these two paragraphs? What kinds of questions might propel the reader, full of curiosity, to read further? Well, for one, who is Dill? And why did he want Boo Radley to come out? And, now that I think about it, why won't Boo Radley come out? These are natural questions that pique the curiosity in the reader, encouraging him to turn the page.

Ask yourself these questions about the book you selected from your bookshelf:

- What did you learn about the character in this scene?
- How does the author hint (or overtly state) the complications that will arise in this novel?
- What do you know about the plot so far?
- Do you feel drawn into the story? Why?
- What is the significance of the starting point?

And then, of course, you'll want to apply these questions to your own work. Have you begun your novel in the right place? I can't tell you how many times I've read my students' work that should have really begun several pages into the story. Ask yourself this question: If I had to start my story at a different point in my narrative, where would it be? Is there any way I can begin closer to the conflict?

Anton Chekhov famously advised his students to tear their stories in half and begin in the middle. What might be a secondary starting place for you?

Last week you reread your novel and made a reverse outline, assessing the value and the worth of each individual scene. Hopefully, this exercise helped you figure out what was working and what wasn't—and in no place is this more important than right out of the gate in your starting scene. Spend some time reworking the first scene of your novel, paying particular attention to grabbing your reader's attention immediately. Save the flowery prose or long, detailed descriptions of setting for another chapter. Instead get your reader immediately invested in your novel through your characters and the story. In the aggregate, these two elements, character and story, are what make for memorable novels.

WEEK 12, ASSIGNMENT 2: *The Riveting Reflective Finale*
Because you just spent some time thinking about your beginning, and since endings should in some way connect back to your novel's opening pages, now would be an excellent time to think about how you decided to end your novel. But first, go back to that book you selected for the last assignment, and read the last few paragraphs. Then ask yourself these questions:

- How is the ending connected to the beginning?
- What has your character seemed to learn?
- What is the tone of the ending?
- What is the "overall" feel of the final paragraphs?

Let's take another look at *Memoirs of a Geisha*. Even if you've never read the book, you can clearly see how the ending mirrors the beginning:

It's true that sometimes when I cross Park Avenue, I'm struck with the peculiar sense of how exotic my surroundings are. The yellow taxicabs that go sweeping past, honking their horns; the women with their briefcases, who look so perplexed to see a little old Japanese woman standing on the street corner in kimono. But really, would Yoroido seem any less exotic if I went back there again? As a young girl, I believed my life would never have been a struggle if Mr. Tanaka hadn't torn me away from my tipsy house. But now I know that our world is no more permanent than a wave rising in the ocean. Whatever our struggles and triumphs, however we may suffer them, all too soon they bleed into a wash, just watery ink on paper.

This ending, like many novel endings, is reflective in tone, which is something you should be mindful of in your own work. Endings should not mimic the finale of a fireworks show or a musical overture, where the most bravado is saved for the final few moments. Instead your readers want a sense of how the world has changed for your protagonist or how your protagonist has been changed by the world. What has been learned? More importantly, what has been the point of his journey—and your novel, by extension? While you want to avoid being overtly didactic by force-feeding your readers a universal message, you do want to hint at what has been learned and what the themes of your novel might be. The narrator above has learned of the impermanence of the world, and this has been a cathartic release for her. Struggles, pain, and even triumphs all fade away, and so one must not wallow in the past.

Also notable: This ending mirrors the first paragraphs in content and tone. The narrator remains, as in the opening paragraph, casually conversational. Additionally, the novel begins with a reference to Mr. Tanaka and ends—as you might have guessed—with a reference to Mr. Tanaka. This repetition gives a feeling of closure to the novel, a feeling of coming full circle.

To Kill a Mockingbird also connects back to the introductory paragraphs with its final words.

> "An' they chased him 'n' never could catch him 'cause they didn't know what he looked like, an' Atticus, when they finally saw him, why he hadn't done any of those things ... Atticus, he was real nice...."
>
> His hands were under my chin, pulling up the cover, tucking it around me.
>
> "Most people are, Scout, when you finally see them."
>
> He turned out the light and went to Jem's room. He would be there all night, and he would be there when Jem waked up in the morning.

In this final brief exchange between Atticus and Scout, the reader understands what Scout, whose words initially beckon us into this novel on those first pages, has learned. The message is simple, though timeless: People aren't always what they appear. This message, clearly one aimed at Boo Radley himself, connects us back to the first pages when we learned about this same character who wouldn't come out of his self-imposed reclusion.

Some people say that if your first scene sells your first novel, your final scene sells your next one. While I certainly don't advise you to begin thinking about selling a second novel before you've even finished the current project, I do think these words can help you weigh the importance of your novel's ending. The final pages will help your characters live on, even after the reader has closed the book. How do you want them to be remembered?

Read your conclusion side by side with your introduction and ask yourself the following questions:

- Is my conclusion reflective in tone?
- Does my conclusion reveal what my character has learned or how he has changed?
- Does my conclusion make a clear link or reference back to the introduction in order to give the novel a feeling of cohesiveness?
- Does my concluding scene imply what my character wants for the future?

Spend some time revising your final scene, paying attention to crafting a concluding scene that connects with your opening scene. The last scene of your novel will linger in your readers' minds.

WEEK 12, ASSIGNMENT 3: *Theme Me Up, Scotty*

As you know by now, not just anybody can write. Or, rather, not just anybody can write well. Think about your friends and family. Who are the best storytellers or joke tellers? Who knows how to keep an audience listening? Who tells stories that drag on and on and on, and you want to scream, *Get to the point, Grandma!* But you know you can't because Grandma's jaw would drop to the floor, along with her dentures. My own granny, on the other hand, used to spin a tale that would keep everyone leaning toward her, as though just by getting closer, we'd hear the next part faster. She was always pausing dramatically for effect, to heighten our anticipation, and she'd make wild facial expressions that would serve as quasi illustrations. Granny had yards of yarn to spin about her life and adventures.

But writing a novel is a bit different than just telling a story. It's about making connections; it's about developing characters and deepening conflicts. It's about providing miniature snapshots that add up to a fully realized collage. But, as you know by now, too, your novel's got to have heart in order to connect with your readers.

Fitzgerald once wrote in a letter to a friend, "That is part of the beauty of all literature. You discover that your longings are universal longings, that you're not lonely and isolated from anyone. You belong." Anyone who has been an avid lifelong reader understands this notion. As a child, some of my greatest friends seemed to be characters in the books I'd read, and these characters were kind enough to let me tag along on their adventures with them (even when my older siblings would not). This is the real appeal of reading novels—to lose ourselves in a world that is totally different from our own, yet one that provides us a universal understanding of how *our* world works. What we're really talking about now is yet another literary device: theme.

The theme of your novel is the fundamental, universal message you want your reader to take away from your story. It's the big-picture idea, the beach that your novel's grain of sand represents. Those who claim that the theme of a novel is whatever a reader takes away from it are, in my opinion, full of hooey. (How's that for a grandmotherly expression?) Certain themes are clearly supported by a close reading of a novel in a way that other themes aren't. *The Great Gatsby* doesn't contain the theme that love conquers all, for instance. No reading of the characters, their intentions, dialogue, or plot possibly indicates this. No, instead all authors, including Fitzgerald, clearly intend for certain themes to come across in their books through their use of character development, imagery, symbols or symbolic moments, or poignant, poetic lines of prose and dialogue. Generations of readers remember that green light at the end of Daisy's dock across the water from Gatsby's mansion. And it's this same water that separates East from West Egg that prompts Nick Carraway to ruminate in the final lines of the book, "So we beat on, boats against the current, borne back ceaselessly into the past." (Did you answer the pop quiz correctly from two weeks ago?) The green light, the poetry, the water, the theme—it's all connected.

Now that you've written a working draft of your novel, it's important for you to clarify and reveal your intended themes in the novel. The climax should dramatize the themes of your work, but several of your other scenes should deepen the themes in more subtle ways, such as through a character description, the use of a minor character, a particularly illuminating image, a clearly rendered setting, or a pertinent symbol.

Pretend you are a reader of your novel. First, write a short essay (no more than five hundred words) that explores the theme(s) of your novel-in-progress. Where do you see evidence of this theme? Be specific. There won't be extra credit.

Now revise a minimum of three scenes—your novel's climax and two others of your choosing—with a specific and critical eye toward further developing your themes. What do you want your readers to take away from your work? What are the universal messages that will speak to your readers and make them feel as though they belong? After all, that's the beauty of a novel—making a solitary reader feel as if she's among friends.

CLEANING UP YOUR ACTS

It's hard to believe that nearly three months ago you signed a contract with yourself and wrote the first sentence of your novel. Here you are now, maybe tired, maybe worn, but, hopefully, thankful that you saw this project through to completion. You've accomplished an enormous amount of work in that short time, and you've created an entire fictional world, populated with interesting characters you've likely come to care about deeply. You've told the best story you can, and that is, after all, the goal of a fiction writer. You're proud of yourself, and you have every right to be. Not just anybody can write a novel: It can be a physically, mentally, and emotionally taxing process, and the benefits don't always outweigh the rewards. Heck, why am I telling *you* this? You know firsthand now.

By now, you are really, really, really ready to hit the print button on your computer and send out as many copies as you can find readers. It's a natural inclination. You feel you've finished something worthwhile, something you put time, energy, and sacrifice into, and you want to share it with the world, like, ASAP. Your novel is like a newborn child, and you are a smiling, doting parent, fit to burst with pride. You want validation for all your work. I know the feeling. While you may be tempted to shirk off the assignments for these final days—you do, after all, have a working draft of your novel ready for some outside readers—I caution you not to be too eager before you've paid at least some attention to editing your work.

Why? Well, I guess there is something I should have told you right from the start....

First drafts, though often well-conceived, well-written, well-plotted pieces of craft, are seldom publishable as is. As mentioned earlier, the difference between a good novel and a great one is the difference between writing and rewriting. And rewriting, just like the initial drafting, can be hard work, too. I tell you all of this not to discourage you, but, on the contrary, to encourage you to become a keen self-editor. The more outwardly polished your draft, the easier it will be for your readers to forget they are reading and lose themselves in your fictional world.

Or think of it like this: A tailor has been commissioned by the queen to make her a cloak. He spends hours toiling away, thimble-thumbed, making sure the cut is right, the quality is good, and the design is flawless. Is he finished once the final seam is sewn up? Heck, no! That's when he begins embellishing the royal cloak with diamond-plated buttons, decorative gold stitching, a collar made of the finest mink fur (faux, of course, since our queen belongs to PETA). The tailor knows that it's not just how well made the cloak is, but how outwardly beautiful it appears when he presents it to Her Majesty at the Royal Cloaking Ceremony.

Before we go further, it's important to define the distinction between self-editing and revising. The two are often conflated, though they are distinct (yet interrelated) concepts. Revising asks you to look at your novel as a whole: Which scenes work, which scenes don't? Where does your plot lose steam? How can you further develop your character or reveal his motivations? These are the kinds of questions you want to ask yourself when you revise your essay.

Editing is a similar enterprise yet focuses a bit more on the discrete elements of fiction that make up the whole of your novel: Where does your voice sound "off"? Where does your point of view get confusing? Where can a bit of description aid in clarity? How can you reorder some of your scenes for a more streamlined novel? Where does a character act out of character? Editing is not simply proofreading your work for typos, though many people confuse the two. While proofreading is absolutely essential before sending out your manuscript, editing deals with more global issues, such as consistency, clarity, conciseness, and correctness (The 4 C's, as taught to me by one of my mentors). It's a process of critique.

Side note: Trust me, a typo-riddled manuscript won't get past the slush pile; it's akin to sending a cover letter that states, "Hello, I'm a lazy, sloppy writer, and I haven't bothered to learn the rules. Please publish my manuscript." If you don't know all the rules of punctuation, look it up.

> Typo's aredistracting. You're writting is a reflextion of you.

If you're not a good proofreader, hire one. Proofreading rates are relatively cheap—and worth it if you're serious about your work. That is all. End of side note.

In the remaining days, I want to pay close attention to some core techniques of editing. In fact, I want you to hire yourself during these last days to be your best self-editor. This is going to take a great deal of self-criticism on your part. You, meet You. Now decide upon a fair pay rate for yourself, exchange drafts, and get to work.

THE HOMESTRETCH, ASSIGNMENT 1:
Your First Job as Editor: Judging a Book by Its Cover

Your first job as your own hired editor is to make sure your novel's plot is substantial enough to sustain the interest of your reader. While we've already attended to this concept a great deal in the outline-creation phase, your final product may differ dramatically from the outline you used to get there. You'll want to double-check, before you ask others to read your work, that your work contains a story worthy of a novel-length work.

Go to your bookshelf right now and select a book at random. Now read the back-cover copy, otherwise known as the book's description or marketing pitch (sometimes this copy is located on the inside flap of the book). Then answer the following questions: What is the main conflict in this novel? Will this one main conflict open up the door to other conflicts? Will this plot offer a range of experiences and emotions for the reader? How might this story appeal on a universal level to the audience? No need to open the book; I'm simply asking you to judge the book by the (copy on the) cover.

I selected the novel *Housekeeping* by Marilynne Robinson. The back cover reads:

> *Housekeeping* is the story of Ruth and her younger sister, Lucille, who grow up haphazardly, first under the care of their competent grandmother, then of two comically bumbling great-aunts, and finally of Sylvie, their eccentric and remote aunt. The family house is in the small Far West town of Fingerbone, which is set on a glacial lake, the same lake

> where their grandfather died in a spectacular train wreck
> and their mother drove off a cliff to her death....Ruth and
> Lucille's struggle toward adulthood beautifully illuminates
> the price of loss and survival, and the dangerous and deep
> undertow of transience.

Even if you've never read *Housekeeping,* just from the back-cover copy, you get a general understanding of the book. Ruth and Lucille have lost their mother, and afterward they are raised by a series of relatives, some more suited for guardianship than others. From this back-cover copy alone, we have a sense of characters, conflict, setting, and theme, and we know the universal message will fall in the general category of "loss and survival," a theme many readers can relate to, for obvious reasons. Further, the very idea of "loss and survival" hints at a range of emotions: Loss insinuates sadness, while survival implies themes more uplifting in nature.

Write your own back-cover copy in about one hundred words. What are the major plot points and conflicts? Who are your major characters? Then honestly answer these questions: Why do you think your story is interesting? Why do you think it's appealing? Who do you think this book will appeal to?

You may find, upon editorial inspection, that your story doesn't have as broad an appeal as you'd originally imagined it to have. If this is the case, it'll be important for you to reexamine your novel and make some changes. Sometimes broadening the appeal can be a simple fix—such as manipulating the ending or giving your character a different occupation or providing a backstory.

Additionally, writing the back-cover copy will also ensure you've begun your novel in the correct place, for it

The Homestretch

CLEANING UP YOUR ACTS

253

forces you to think about what is essential for your reader to know. For example, if your back-cover copy begins, "On the day of her wedding, Poppy jumped from the third-floor balcony, ran into town, and took a bus that would change her life forever...." it's likely that you don't need to begin your novel during Poppy's childhood on an asparagus farm in California.

Writing your back-cover copy helps you think about the marketing of your novel—though, to be clear, this isn't your job as a novelist. Nor do I want you to concern yourself very much with marketing your novel. Not while you're here in your writing zone. But marketing, in general, concerns itself with connecting a message to an audience in a way that appeals to an audience. And this is your concern as a writer, too. On a simple level, who would be most interested in Poppy's story? Does it have enough universal appeal? Is your conflict clearly stated? These are big questions to address at this late stage in the game, but they're probably the first ones that a book editor would ask.

THE HOMESTRETCH, ASSIGNMENT 2:
The Final Read-Through and a Self-Editing Checklist

A couple of weeks ago, you were asked to read through the entire draft of your novel in order to reverse outline it. Since then, you've been revising, editing, and polishing your work. One final time, I want you to print out a copy of your novel, find a quiet place, and read your novel from start to finish. The read will go relatively quickly because you're so familiar with your recent work, so try to do it in one sitting. As you're reading, I want you to accomplish several things listed on this self-editor's checklist:

1. Notice how much tactile, physical description you use. Where could you use more? Where are you being abstract? Remember, just because something is clear in your mind doesn't mean it's clear in the mind of your reader. Avoid abstractions, being overly general, or too internal. Aim for a minimum of one bit of physical description on every page. For example, the room was hot—and painted hot pink.

2. Circle or otherwise indicate any sections of your novel where you got bored or found yourself skimming paragraphs. Trust me: If you grow bored with your own work, your readers will, too. How can you make these sections more interesting? Can you afford to cut these parts? If so, I'd advise you to do it.

3. Where is your reader given information about your characters' histories? Is it enough to really know your character? Where could you give more insight in the past experiences, histories, and motivations of your characters?

4. Which of your minor characters (if any) don't seem to be serving any real purpose? Sometimes you can simply combine two characters into one in order to remedy this problem. For instance, if three bumbling cops arrive at the scene of the crime, yet only one cop actually interacts with your protagonist, condense these characters into one bumbling police officer. Make every character count, but do not overlap their purposes.

5. Which is your favorite scene in the novel? Why is it your favorite? What do you do particularly well that you could mimic in other scenes, too? Analyze what you've done well in this scene and apply these techniques to other scenes of your work.

6. Read your dialogue out loud to see if it sounds realistic. Do your characters sound different enough from one

another? Where does the dialogue sound contrived? Since I can't be there with you to make sure you're reading out loud, I'm going to hold you to the honor system. Reading your work out loud—and not just the dialogue—is an excellent way to pick up on tonal issues in your prose. I'd strongly recommend reading your entire work out loud before you submit it to an editor. This is a trick of many published writers, and perhaps one reason why they are published in the first place.

7. Do any single scenes feel like they are lacking a beginning, a middle, or an end? Remember, each scene itself should feel like a completed snapshot, not just a hastily drawn vignette.

8. Have you described, or at least noted, the setting of every scene? You'd be surprised how easy it is to pass over the description of place when you write. Perhaps this is because we can see things so clearly in our heads. Make sure each scene is clearly set.

9. Remember our discussion of active versus passive verbs way back on Day 2? Almost three months have passed since then, so flip back to that day's lesson, if need be. When you use active voice, the subject of the sentence is doing the action; in passive voice, the subject receives the action. Do you notice yourself using a lot of "be" verbs in your novel (*am, is, are, was, were, being, been*)? If you overuse them, make the necessary fixes. Eliminating the overuse of these verbs will make your writing more lively, vivid, and colorful.

10. This last assignment will be difficult for you, but it's good practice for learning to let go. Find at least three whole paragraphs in your novel and delete them. Part ways with at least three paragraphs. Why? Because we must always

learn to trim back on our writing, and it's an important lesson to learn where you can cut chunks of your work in order to strengthen your plot. You may feel attached to every word you've written the past three months, but force yourself to do it. I have no doubt you'll be able to find at least three paragraphs that aren't doing much work in your novel. No cheating. If you're really attached to your words, save these paragraphs and use them down the road in a different novel/story.

THE HOMESTRETCH, ASSIGNMENT 3: *Finding Your Critics, or, "Just Say No" to Relatives as Final Readers*

You've come a long way, baby. Through hard work, diligence, and habit, you turned the kernel of an idea into a novel, and it only took you ninety days. Congratulations. You've joined the club populated only by a fraction of the population with enough discipline and dedication to write a book. You are now a novelist, even if you never write another word in your life. But let's hope that's not the case. I like to think of a first novel as practice for a second, and a second novel as practice for the third. If you remember Malcolm Gladwell's idea that it takes ten thousand hours to become an expert on anything, you've probably put in only a fraction of that time on this project. With practice, time, and honesty, you'll become a better and better writer. The key is this: Never give up.

You've completed your novel, but if your end goal is to publish your work, you don't want to query agents and editors just yet. (We'll be discussing that process in the final chapter.) Before you begin to query agents and editors, you'll want to find some outside readers who will give you an unbiased, objective opinion about your work. Did you notice I said *unbiased and objective?* By definition, then, this means you shouldn't ask your family members, spouse, or partner to read and give critical feedback on your work. Please, please, please don't select readers who are related to you through blood or marriage. Why? Because your husband is not unbiased. He loves you, and rightly so. Neither is your mother-in-law unbiased. Your partner doesn't want to upset you either, knowing you've just spent hours a day, for months, writing this book. She's not going to be the one to dampen your dreams with some of her suggestions. From these people, bless their hearts, you'll likely hear: *It's great! I love it! Wow, you wrote that? I'm so impressed you wrote an entire novel. That's so cool!* And they may mean it. Or they may not mean it. That's the problem with asking feedback from someone who loves us; most of the time we just can't tell their level of "truthiness." (Props, Stephen Colbert.)

Look, I'm not saying these people can't read your work. *Of course* you can let them read it. It's part of you now, just as much as that mole on your neck (the one you prefer to call a beauty mark). But don't expect any useful criticism from these individuals unless they happen to be editors themselves. When I say that you should find outside readers, I am suggesting you find readers who will be willing and unafraid to give you the honest feedback that very well might … hurt your feelings. Your feelings will get hurt. Why? Because at this point, after you've spent ninety days working on a novel, you feel the work is a part of you. And, well, it is, in a way. But you've got to toughen your skin, stiffen your upper lip. You won't become a better writer without constructive criticism.

The good news is there are several ways to find objective outside readers. If you're willing to pay a modest fee, one suggestion is to query a local college or university's English department. Department administrators are usually more than willing to post a call for a reader on the department Listserv, and plenty of poor graduate students would welcome the opportunity to make a couple of extra bucks reading your manuscript. I know firsthand. I used to be one of these poor graduate students who edited and critiqued the work of strangers for some extra cash.

If you're not comfortable with this idea, you should consider joining a local writers' group, if you're not already part of one. You can find announcements for such groups in your local paper, at the library, or even on a site such as Craigslist.com. But be careful! For every one good/productive writers' group, you'll find about ten that aren't useful or constructive. These groups like to sit around and complain and yammer on and on and on about writing instead of doing any writing themselves. Every city has writers' groups—the trick is finding a good one. (Or you could always start one yourself if you know a group of writers looking for a community.)

If all else fails, you can ask a few trusted friends to read your work, though you should select friends who actually read novels in their spare time. Selecting a nonreader as an outside reader would be like going to a dentist for gardening suggestions. It's just not a clear match. You want somebody who knows a bit about writing, and good readers, even if they are not writers themselves, can certainly give you some very useful input.

Keep in mind that you want to make this process as easy for your outside readers as possible. In doing so, you ensure, or at least hope, that they'll give you generous amounts of feedback. You'll want to follow some general guidelines: First, when you give the manuscript to your readers, it should be accompanied by an instruction sheet, and the first instruction should read: BE HONEST. I PROMISE MY FEELINGS WILL NOT BE HURT BY YOUR CRITICISM. (And you should mean these words; don't set your friends up to criticize you and then be angry when they offer criticism. While sensitivity is probably one personal trait that led you to become a writer in the first place, too much sensitivity, especially when your work is criticized, can really stunt your growth as an artist.)

In addition, you should also provide your outside readers a list of questions to read before they've read your novel and to answer once they've finished. This way, they'll know what to look for when they read. The more specific the questions you provide, the more specific your feedback will be. If you just ask your reader for his general feedback, he's likely to say: "It was good." But if you probe him with specific questions such as "Did you feel invested in the main character?" or "Where in the novel did you get bored?" or "Where did you not understand the motivations of the protagonist?" you'll get a much clearer idea of what needs improvement. Here are some sample questions below, but feel free to include your own based on your curiosities and needs:

1. Did you feel invested in the main character?
2. Were you interested in the story? Where did you lose interest or get bored?
3. Which chapters moved too slowly?
4. Did you feel satisfied with the ending?

90 DAYS TO YOUR NOVEL

5. Did you feel you knew enough about the characters' backgrounds to understand the plot?
6. Did you understand the protagonist's motivations?
7. Where was more clarity necessary?
8. Did you find the protagonist a believable character?

It's also a good idea to actually print out the copy of the manuscript for your outside readers. While it does save paper to send copies via electronic copy, it's a different experience reading a novel on paper versus on the screen. Additionally, if your outside readers wish to line edit or write notes in the margins, the process will be much easier for them on printed paper. Again, strive to make this process as easy as possible. These people are, after all, doing you a favor, especially if they don't get paid.

As you know, it's always easier to work with a set deadline. Give your outside readers a deadline, and plan to have a conversation with them in person when they are finished. Keep in mind that you won't always agree with the input of a single individual, which is why it's absolutely necessary to get feedback from more than one person. If all of your readers agree on similar points—say, chapter five was a total dud—then you'll probably want to take this criticism to heart, even if chapter five was your favorite scene in the entire novel.

THE FINAL ASSIGNMENT

You've crossed the finish line. Ninety days ago, you had only the faintest glimmer of an idea about your novel, and today you stand (or sit) here as the proud author of a novel. Doesn't it feel good? Did you think you could do it? Were even *you* impressed with your dedication to the project? You're no longer someone who says she wants to write—you're a writer *because* you write. You took the challenge, dedicated the time, and probably sacrificed a lot in the process. But you realize now how much writers are mythologized. You don't need argyle socks; you don't need dark-rimmed glasses or red wine or a sweater vest or a pipe. These are just props. You don't need to sit in the smokiest of coffee shops, or hope the moody mood lighting of the moodiest place in town is going to inspire you to get writing. Writing is a lonely endeavor, unsexy in every sense of the definition, you now realize—heck, you found yourself writing in your bathrobe and slippers—but it feels really good—great, in fact—when you make progress and fill those empty pages from the ether of your creative mind. I hope by now you've dispelled those erroneous notions of a writer as anything but someone who, day after day, puts pen to paper or fingers to keyboard ... and writes.

Here's your final assignment, after you've had that celebratory drink or treated yourself to a fancy dinner at your favorite joint: Put your work away. You read that correctly. Put your work away for a while. While your novel is off with your outside readers, don't crack a page of your work. Don't change a sentence. Don't read a word. You need perspective, and you won't get it by obsessing. Take a vacation, pick up a hobby, put your computer or your manuscript in a closet, lock it, and hide the key from yourself. Swallow the key, if you must (though I don't suggest that). Watch a movie, learn to juggle, memorize "The Gettysburg Address," and then dress up like Lincoln and deliver it to your family and friends for fun. Do anything but look at your novel for a while.

Then, when enough time has passed, a few weeks at the bare minimum, you can return to your work with fresh eyes and renewed energy. You'll be returning to the novel a new you, one who has not been mired in plot choices, one who has not embodied these characters' minds, and one who has not been living, faithfully, in some imaginary world. You'll be surprised at how much perspective you gain when you give yourself a bit of a break from your work—and this perspective will be crucial to adding those finishing touches.

It's this kind of perspective that turns a novel into a thoughtful meditation on the world. William Faulkner wrote, "The writer's only responsibility is his art." While, over the course of these past ninety days, we've discussed your novel as a joint communion between your novel and a reader, in the end, you must always be true to the artistic vision you originally held—your own green light, perhaps, that keeps you yearning, that keeps you ceaselessly seeking to reinterpret the world through the lens of your fiction.

The Homestretch

DAY 91 AND BEYOND

Finally! You've arrived! I've been waiting here at the finish line, my timer set to ninety days to see if you'd make it on time. The race challenged you on many levels, I'm sure—but you now know that you have what it takes (stamina, determination, work ethic) to be a novel writer. As you crossed the ninety-day mark, did you look and feel a bit like Eric Liddell, the great Scots character from *Chariots of Fire*, your head drawn back, your face contorted with the sheer joy of running? Or did you find yourself clawing the dirt and collapsing only inches past your deadline? Really, it doesn't matter how you finished, it matters that you finished. Bravo. Bravo! Put your ear to this book and let the pages flutter—can you hear the applause?

By this point, copies of your manuscript are off with your designated outside readers, and like a parent who's hired a babysitter to take the kids for an afternoon, you just don't know what to do with all your free time. Don't worry; there's plenty left to consider.

After ninety days of writing and thinking about writing and writing some more, I want you to shift your attention to a different topic altogether: publishing. Publishing is, after all, the end goal of most novelists. (Yes, there are those who say they write because they have to write—it's part of one's identity. These same individuals also happily publish their work when the opportunity arises.)

The world of publishing may feel a bit mysterious to you at this point, scary even, and in this last chapter I want to unravel some of these mysteries. Hopefully, that big scary monster in the window will become something much less frightening in the end—say, a shadow cast from a garden gnome. Once we learn about the way something functions, it becomes much easier to understand the process. I hope this is the case for you, too.

Books are published on the subject of publishing, and you'll find many sources at your fingertips once you start looking. And if you're serious about publishing, you're going to need to do some research. Will you aim for a large, traditional publisher? A small, independent publishing house? Are you interested in self-publishing your novel and trying to distribute it yourself? If a large publishing house publishes your work, the distribution network will be wider, but you'll probably be giving up some of your artistic/editorial rights as the author. Smaller houses are often more nuanced and are willing to compromise with an author once a contract is signed. Smaller houses often afford you more input regarding what the final product will look like. If you don't know much about any of these terms, you'll want to do some research to at least familiarize yourself with the publishing industry. But one thing is for certain: If you want to publish via the traditional route (i.e., through a publisher), you're going to first have to go through either an agent or an editor.

DEMYSTIFYING THE ROLE OF AGENT AND EDITOR

You'll find several paths to publishing your book, and no single path is better than the other. But, first, you'll need to understand a bit about the differences between an agent and an editor. Again, entire books have been written on this subject, and this book focuses mainly on *writing* your novel, so for a more in-depth look at the industry, you may wish to visit your library or local bookstore. The Internet also offers no shortage of information.

An agent functions as a middleman between an editor and an author. So, if you send your novel to an agent, and this agent agrees to represent your work, he or she will then look for an editor for you. The easiest way to think of the job of an agent is to think of the role in terms of a celebrity. Kevin Bacon has an agent, and it's the job of his agent to find his next movie role. And when the agent finds it, he or she gets a certain percentage of Bacon's contract, or, as I like to say, Bacon's bacon. Likewise, if you find an agent who is willing to represent you, he or she will pitch your novel to various editors at numerous publishing houses, trying to find a home for your novel. If your agent does find you a book contract, he'll usually take a standard 15 percent cut of your earnings.

This is the part where you chime in: *If an agent takes 15 percent of my hard-earned money, why not just go directly to an editor? Won't I make more money that way, and won't it streamline the process to query editors directly?* The answer: Not really. (The other answer is that nobody becomes a writer for the money.)

Agents know the market. Agents get paid to know the market. Agents also have a wealth of contacts at multiple publishing houses, and so you're really paying to tap into their network. If your novel will appeal to a particular demographic—say, young adults—your agent will immediately know the names and numbers of editors at a publishing house that specialize in the genre of YA novels. In addition, agents know how to broker contracts, so you can rest assured you'll get the best deal possible. After all, if your agent is going for 15 percent of your book contract, he'll want to get the biggest possible contract for you so that his cut can bring home the bacon, too. An agent represents your novel and saves you, the writer, the time and hassle of pitching your novel directly to editors. Some editors, in fact, will not deal with anyone but an agent. (And what will you do with this freed-up time? You'll write of course!)

But something you need to keep in mind is that even if you query an agent, and even if that agent agrees to represent your work, and even if you sign a contract with your agent, you are still not assured a book deal. If you are a first timer, agents will generally represent your book for a set period of time, perhaps a year, and if that time period elapses with no book deal, your book's representation will be released back to you. It's only fair, after all. If your agent can't find an editor within a year, perhaps you can find a different agent who can.

You should do some serious research before querying agents to represent your novel so you don't waste your time. If you've written a crime novel, you'll want to find an agent who represents other crime writers. If you've written a literary novel, you'll want to find an agent who deals primarily with literary fiction. And so on. Be sure to know your agent's background and terms before you sign your firstborn novel on the dotted line.

If you do decide to forgo the agent and submit directly to editors, you'll want to also do some research about the kind of publishing house each editor represents. An editor, after all, works directly for a publisher. Make a list of your favorite recently published novels and research which publisher published these books. Is the publishing house large or small? Does the publishing house publish only one genre? For instance, if you send your action-packed coming-of-age novel to Harlequin Mills & Boon, you'll likely be immediately rejected without a second glance. Why? Harlequin publishes primarily romance novels. Whether you decide to submit queries to an editor or an agent, do your homework before submitting.

A word about rejections: You'll receive plenty. Think of them as badges of honor. But don't let them discourage you. Every writer receives plenty of rejection slips—many short, impersonal, or arrogant—so prepare yourself for this. I've heard stories of writers who have wallpapered their bathrooms with rejection slips they've received from editors far and wide. Perhaps you could find another use for yours— scrap paper for grocery lists, fire kindling—or simply use them as encouragement to submit again.

In my writing classes, I have my students submit their stories to one of the most prestigious magazines around, let's call it *The Timbuktu Review*, for the sake of anonymity. Do I really think a draft of a student's story will be accepted at *The Timbuktu Review*? No. Do the students think they'll be accepted? No. But I have them do it as an exercise in both submitting and accepting rejections. It's the name of the game, and if you can't accept rejection, you should probably think twice about becoming a writer.

QUERY, MY DEARIE

At the risk of sounding redundant, I'm going to say it again: You need to do your research before contacting agents or editors. You'll need to figure out who is the best agent or editor to represent the novel you've written, and this may take some research.

Once you decide upon an agent or editor, you're going to have to send them a query letter. A query letter is essentially a letter that asks an agent or editor to please take a look at your novel and consider representing it, thank you very much. You'll be much more articulate than that. You should *always* read the guidelines for submitting to either your agent or your editor and follow those guides exactly. For instance, if the submission guidelines ask for a detailed synopsis, send them one. If they ask for a short synopsis, send them that instead. If they ask for only the first ten pages of your novel, be sure to send that. You get the point. Never submit your entire novel manuscript unless you are asked.

Here are some general guidelines for writing and submitting a query letter:

- Keep your letter limited to one page. Do not go over, even if you feel like you have a lot to say. Introduce yourself and your novel and then politely and professionally ask the agent or editor if she'd be interested in reading your novel. Provide your writerly credentials if you have any recent or relevant ones, and don't include any extraneous information. Do not mention that you worked on your high school newspaper. Do not mention that you enjoy scrawling poetry in your free time, particularly poems about your cat Pumpkin.

Query letters never really help you, per se (that is, you won't get published based on your letter), but they can hurt you if you sound unprofessional, needy, whiny, desperate, self-congratulatory, or pathetic.

- Do not try to get creative with your query letters. Tone does not come across well in letter form. When I worked for a literary magazine, you wouldn't believe the creative antics people tried to pull in order to get noticed: photographs, drawings, rhyming couplets, jokes. They did get noticed, right before they got rejected. Query letters are not opportunities to practice creativity. Stay professional in tone, and don't try to pull off anything gimmicky or jokey. Do not try to tell them you are the next Lorrie Moore and that they'd be lucky to represent you. Or that your novel is "just like" the *Harry Potter* series and your twelve-year-old niece thought it was awesome.

- Check your letter for grammar and punctuation. Check it again. Check it again. Check it again. Do not rely on a spell-checker to pick up errors. Typos can particularly annoy an editor, who probably began his career as a proofreader. Don't irritate someone you are trying to convince to publish your work. That's counterproductive.

- Include an SASE (self-addressed, stamped envelop) if the editor requests one. If you fail to do this, you may also fail to hear back from the editor.

REVISE REPRISE

You'll be waiting a while to hear back from the agents and editors you've queried. And in the meantime, once you get feedback from your outside readers, you'll want to continue to revise your work with an eye toward any criticisms or comments you received. Remember, you get only one chance to impress the agent or editor, so you want to submit the very best draft possible. Don't get lazy in the final stretch.

Here are some final questions to ask yourself as you work with your draft:

- Does my novel start in the right place? Can I start further in, closer to the action? (Remember, the faster you get your reader involved in the action of the story, the better.)
- Does each scene have a purpose within the larger scope of my novel?
- Do I write with my senses?
- When writing about emotion, do I avoid stating directly how the character is feeling and instead place emotion inside physical descriptions?
- Have I eliminated any overly vague sections or scenes that don't add much weight to my novel?
- Where can I cut scenes?
- Is my point of view consistent throughout the novel? If my POV is from more than one character's head, does this ever get confusing?
- Does my dialogue sound believable, and does it reveal the idiosyncrasies of my character? Have I read my dialogue out loud to see what it sounds like?
- Does my ending resist predictability? Does it feel deserved? Will my reader be happy?

Of course, you can read checklist after checklist after checklist after checklist—but it won't mean anything if you don't actually apply the necessary work to your novel-in-progress. Remember: Revision isn't simply about adding content, it's about deleting content that doesn't strengthen the overall arc of your story. The toughest moment you'll have—and you'll have many of them, if you find excellent, trusted readers—is removing something you like, but that they really *don't like*. Learning to be wrong sometimes, self-correcting, and moving forward with confidence again are some of the most difficult lessons for a new or continuing writer to learn.

They're some of life's lessons, also, to be sure, in the abstract, but they're difficult to internalize if you're emotionally involved with your written words. "But that's how it happened!" is not an acceptable response when your trusted reader confesses they were bored by the deathbed scene of the beloved grandma. (She passed out clippings of her hair like dear Eva did in *Uncle Tom's Cabin*. Then she sighed, pointed toward the sky, said, "To the mooooooon...!" and expired.) If something so dramatic for you isn't getting through to your reader, you need to describe something differently, unearth a better example, or simply start that section from scratch. Maybe your sister ruining your favorite shirt she borrowed without asking wasn't the climactic fight of your childhood after all. And when you really think about it, it's no wonder your reader was bored. Stealing a shirt isn't really that much of a loss. But stealing your childhood love—that's what really smarted. Maybe write that in, but leave the shirt out.

AND THEN SUBMIT

You'll have to wait weeks—months in most cases—to hear back from the agent or editor you queried. You'll likely receive some neatly typed form rejections that are polite and wish you luck placing the novel elsewhere. Do not get discouraged. That is an order, and one of my last ones. The key to publishing is persistence. What separates serious writers from hobbyists is faith in their art.

In the best-case scenario, however, you'll receive a letter asking you to send your novel, or a portion of your novel, for review. This is the news all novelists wait to hear. Woot-woot! Here comes the gravy train! Well, maybe. It's a step in the right direction, at least.

You should put the necessary care into submitting your manuscript for review. And, of course, follow the specific guidelines set by whoever is requesting your work. If they ask for only the first fifty pages, do not send them the entire manuscript. If they ask for the first chapter, don't send them chapters one through three because you think chapter one doesn't really get into the heart of your story. Also, keep in mind these suggestions:

- Do not try to typeset your manuscript using special software. I've seen this many times. Don't try to make an unpublished work look published. This will scream "Amateur!" and it will scream it loudly.
- Your manuscript should be typed in an easy-to-read twelve-point font, and it should be double-spaced with one-inch margins. Make sure your printer has enough ink—nothing worse than trying to read a manuscript from a faded printer. Also, make sure your manuscript is clean—avoid eating peanut-butter-and-jelly sandwiches while stuffing the envelope.
- Include your name and page number in the header of every page in case pages are lost.

- Double-check to make sure all the pages have printed, and make sure no blank pages have been inserted into your printed document. Home printers, especially, are notorious for tucking blank pages within documents.
- Do not bind your manuscript or place in a binder. This is bulky and will cost you more money. And, in all likelihood, the editor or agent will take the manuscript out of the binder before reading. If you feel you *must* bind it because of your obsession with order, put a small rubber band around your manuscript.
- Include a brief cover letter with your manuscript reminding the editor or agent of your past correspondence (i.e., the fact that they asked you to submit) and a reminder about your novel (the title) and your credentials (if you have any). Sound thankful, but do not fall all over yourself with thanks. One "thanks" will suffice. Keep the tone professional. They've asked you to send a manuscript, not to become their friend.

THIS IS THE END

I hope this book has a happy ending; I entrust it to you. We've spent ninety days together, and you either have or haven't proved that you've got what it takes to write a novel. The line in the sand has been crossed, or it hasn't. What else is left to say? Lucky for you, I've saved the best part for last.

The best part is this: Tomorrow is still another day, another opportunity to write, and another chance to construct fictional worlds that lend meaning to our own.

Saul Bellow once said, "A novel is a balance between a few true impressions and the multitude of false ones that make up most of what we call life. It tells us that for every

human being there is a diversity of existences, that the single existence is itself an illusion in part ... it promises us
meaning, harmony, and even justice." Creating a new existence—a reflection, in part, of our lived one—is the greatest aspiration of any fiction writer—and the greatest hope
for what the novel can do.

So, you thought you could write a novel, huh? I always
knew you could. Ninety days is a quick pace but not the
fastest a novel has ever been penned. And, in the long run,
the number of days you spent writing your novel won't
matter; what's most important is you've proven you could
do it. What matters most is your book, your artful meditation on the world.

Congratulations on your novel—and happy writing.

ACKNOWLEDGEMENTS

This book would not be possible without the advice of some of my excellent writing teachers and mentors along the way, in particular Brock Clarke, Michael Griffith, and Nicola Mason. Thanks to Kelly Nickell, Scott Francis, and Kim Catanzarite for their sharp editorial insights in shaping this book. Thanks to my friends Lauren Mosko Bailey, Jana Braziel, Kelcey Parker, Jody Bates, and Julie Gerk-Hernandez for innumerable conversations about writing and teaching (and life) that have inspired me. Thanks to the members of the inaugural 90 Days to Your Novel writers' group for their commiseration with the experiment. Special gratitude to my family, especially my parents for their wisdom and unconditional support, and to Mary Ann, Luke, Laura, Jeff, Shelby, Angelina, and Eli for surrounding me with their friendship and laughter. And lastly, but firstly and always, my gratitude and love to my beloved first reader, Robert B. Seal. I'll always be thankful.

ABOUT THE AUTHOR

Sarah Domet's fiction and nonfiction appears in *New Delta Review*, *The Cincinnati Review*, *Beloit Fiction Journal*, *Potomac Review*, *Harpur Palate*, and *Many Mountains Moving*. She holds a Ph.D. in comparative literature and fiction from the University of Cincinnati and currently teaches in the writing department at Georgia Southern University. For more information, visit her Web site at www. sarahdomet.com.

INDEX

278